CONSIDER THIS

CONSIDER THIS

Moments in My Writing Life

after Which Everything Was Different

CHUCK PALAHNIUK

GC

GRAND CENTRAL
PUBLISHING

NEW YORK   BOSTON

Grand Central Publishing
Hachette Book Group
1290 Avenue of the Americas, New York, NY 10104
grandcentralpublishing.com
twitter.com/grandcentralpub

First edition: January 2020

Grand Central Publishing is a division of Hachette Book Group, Inc. The
Grand Central Publishing name and logo is a trademark of Hachette
Book Group, Inc.

The publisher is not responsible for websites (or their content) that are
not owned by the publisher.

The Hachette Speakers Bureau provides a wide range of authors for
speaking events. To find out more, go to
www.hachettespeakersbureau.com or call (866) 376-6591.

Library of Congress Cataloging-in-Publication Data has been applied for.

ISBNs: 978-1-5387-1795-0 (hardcover), 978-1-5387-1796-7 (ebook)

Book design by Sean Ford

Printed in the United States of America

LSC-C

10   9   8   7   6   5   4   3   2

To Tom Spanbauer with
gratitude and respect

Contents

CONTENTS

Author's Note

This book contains the best advice and stories of many brilliant people. Most are credited, two are not. Those two are Wes Miller, who edited the manuscript for Grand Central; and Scott Allie, who edited the manuscript a year before Wes saw it, and later arranged for the tattoo illustrations. What works here works with their considerable help.

A second helping of my appreciation goes out to Sara Reinhart for helping manage the illustrations, and to the artist Toby Linwood at Tattoo 34 in Portland. Don't just get inked, get Toby.

Introduction

For most of my life I haven't balanced my checkbook. The result was too depressing, to find out how little money I'd saved. What little the years of my life had amounted to.

So long as my checks cleared, I'd no interest in figuring down to the penny how poor I always was. For the same reason, I've put off writing a book on writing. I didn't want to be faced with how little I could offer on the subject. How stupid I remained after all this time and practice.

My education consists of a kitchen-table MFA, earned sitting around Andrea Carlisle's kitchen, then Tom Spanbauer's kitchen, then Suzy Vitello's and Chelsea Cain's. My program began in 1988 and continues to this day. There's no graduation ceremony and no diploma.

The first writing workshop I joined was Andrea's, and it consisted of nice people. After a couple of years Andrea took me aside. That week I'd submitted a scene depicting a young man who struggled to complete sex with a slowly deflating sex doll. A scene I'd eventually use in my novel *Snuff*, fifteen years later. On behalf of the other writers Andrea told me I wasn't a good fit for the group. Due to my fiction, no one felt safe around me. As consolation she suggested I study with another writer, Tom Spanbauer. He'd recently moved to Portland from New York.

Tom. Tom's workshop was different. We met in a condemned house he'd bought with plans for renovation. We felt like outlaws just by violating the yellow UNSAFE DO NOT ENTER notice stapled to the door. The previous owner had been a recluse who'd lined the interior with sheets of clear plastic and kept the air constantly warm and misted so he could grow a vast collection of orchids. The house had rotted from the inside out, leaving only a few floorboards that could still support a person's weight. The writer Monica Drake recalls the first time she arrived for a class there and found that all the porches had collapsed. She wandered around the outside, stumped as to how to reach any of the doors that hung high above the junky, overgrown yard. For Monica that impossible leap over broken glass and rusted nails has always stood for the challenge of becoming a professional writer.

About the yard, Tom told us that cutting the blackberry canes and carting away the heaps of garbage would bond us as a team. It wasn't enough to arrive with manuscripts for review. We should also spend our weekends digging up the jagged soup cans and dead cats and carting all of these to a landfill. What did we know? As twenty-somethings we played along, and Tom made us soggy tuna fish sandwiches for lunch. His actual workshop sessions were more conventional, but just slightly. If we found ourselves stuck creatively he might break out the I Ching coins or refer us to his favorite psychic in Seattle. He brought in writers, among them Peter Christopher and Karen Karbo, who could teach us what he could not. What took place was less a class than it was a dialogue. And that's what I'd like this book to be: a dialogue. This isn't just me telling you this. To give credit where it's due, this is my teachers and their teachers' teachers, going back to the caveman days. These are lessons that daisy-chain into the past and the future. They should be organized and curated, by me or by someone.

Still, I'm torn.

One factor pushing me to write this book is a memory of The Worst Writing Workshop Ever. It was taught by a West Coast editor who solicits students by mail. His glossy pamphlets tout him as a sort of Editor to the Stars, listing the legendary dead writers he claims to have groomed from sows' ears into silk purses.

The grooming costs each aspiring student several thousand dollars, payable weeks in advance. The Editor to the Stars swans into the host city for a three-day weekend, staying in a luxury hotel and teaching in a hotel conference room. Needless to say, the only people who can afford his rates are wealthy. Mostly they're the wives of wealthy men, with a couple of tenured college professors thrown into the mix—and me. At each of our three sessions students assembled, read their work, and waited. Everyone looked to the Editor to the Stars, who would sigh deeply and ask us to comment on the work in question.

This strategy allowed the other students to feel smart while it ran out the clock. Opinions flew, but not much practical advice. Usually no practical advice. Opinions collided, and the cross talk ate up more time. During this heated gabfest, the Editor to the Stars was updating his own mailing lists, glancing at messages on his phone, nodding sagely.

In the final moments of debate, the Editor would weigh in with some variation of, "This amusing piece shows a great deal of sensitivity, you should expand it into a novel." Or, "Your work is as promising as [insert some dead writer the Editor claims to have discovered and nurtured to greatness: Hemingway, Faulkner, Harriet Beecher Stowe]. Please keep at it."

Lots of hand-holding. Loads of flattery. By Sunday afternoon each of his twenty-five students had gotten a nice pat on the head but no useful information. And the Editor to the Stars left town forty thousand dollars richer.

After witnessing that racket I'd resolved to write a book. Someday. A tough-love manual with more practical information than a dozen price-gouging writing gurus would typically provide. Still, I'm conflicted.

Holding me back are the dead people. As I take stock of the people who've helped me, the booksellers and fellow writers, I find so many have died. I love knowing a lot of people, but the downside is that means going to a lot of funerals. To write this book would be to pay a debt to those people. But it would be a sad task.

Another reason not to move forward is my best teacher. At this writing, Tom Spanbauer has given up teaching. He tells me that he feels like a fraud. For three decades he's held out the idea that regular people, people with daytime jobs, people from blue-collar families, could write stories that would reach the world. Many of his students have succeeded, including Monica Drake, Stevan Allred, Joanna Rose, Jennifer Lauck, and myself. But Tom's own career has languished, and to him the fiction-teaching routine has begun to look like a scam.

There's more to it. Tom's health isn't the best. But that's too personal to tackle here.

Tom teaches students practical, effective techniques that instantly make their work better. Many of these he learned from the famous editor and writer Gordon Lish. Tom steers readers toward the best writers to emulate. He helps connect his students with agents and editors. And he did this in his own condemned home, every week, since 1990, when he charged each of his students twenty dollars each session. Yet he's honest enough to worry about their chances for success in the bookselling world.

Contrast that with the Editor to the Stars who charges thousands. Ignores his students' work. Knows them for three days. Tells them they're brilliant and that the publishing world is their oyster, then skips town, never to be seen again.

If I'm going to write this book, I want to err on the side of pessimism.

If you're dedicated to becoming an author, nothing I can say here will stop you. But if you're not, nothing I can say will make you one.

*   *   *

That said, if you came to me and asked me to teach you everything I'm able, I'd tell you that the publishing industry is on life support. Bret Easton Ellis tells me the novel is no longer even a blip in the culture. You're too late. Piracy has destroyed the profits. Readers have all moved on to watching films and playing computer games. I'd say, "Kid, go home!"

No one is born to do this job. Storytelling, yes. But when you become an author you seek out other authors the way an Anne Rice vampire seeks vampires as mentors. I was lucky. My first book was endorsed by four great writers: Robert Stone, Katherine Dunn, Thom Jones, and Barry Hannah. Under the pretense of thanking them, I stalked them. Stone came to Portland as part of a panel discussion about Zelda Fitzgerald. When I met him at the Heathman Hotel he told me, "For anything to endure it must be made of either granite or words."

This book is, in a way, a scrapbook of my writing life. From shopping the cathedral flea market in Barcelona with David Sedaris to having drinks at Cognac with Nora Ephron just months before she died. To the years of sporadic correspondence I had with Thom Jones and Ira Levin. I've stalked my share of mentors, asking for advice.

Therefore, if you came back another day and asked me to teach you, I'd tell you that becoming an author involves more than talent and skill. I've known fantastic writers who never finished a project. And writers who launched incredible ideas, then never fully executed them. And I've seen

Robert Stone

writers who sold a single book and became so disillusioned by the process that they never wrote another. I'd paraphrase the writer Joy Williams, who says that writers must be smart enough to hatch a brilliant idea—but dull enough to research it, keyboard it, edit and re-edit it, market the manuscript, revise it, revise it, re-revise it, review the copy edit, proofread the typeset galleys, slog through the interviews and write the essays to promote it, and finally to show up in a dozen cities and autograph copies for thousands or tens of thousands of people…

And then I'd tell you, "Now get off my porch."

But if you came back to me a third time, I'd say, "Kid…" I'd say, "Don't say I didn't warn you."

A Postcard from the Tour

Bob Maull scared the crap out of me. He stood maybe chest high to most people and had a mop of white-gray hair and a walrus mustache. He owned 23rd Avenue Books in Portland, Oregon, and had founded the Pacific Northwest Booksellers Association. Once you're published and trying to scratch out a living you'll find these regional bookseller associations are a great ally. In August 1996 when *Fight Club* was published in hardcover I signed copies at his shop. He took me aside and said, "Kid…"

I was thirty-four and still working full-time at Freightliner Trucks. On the truck assembly line, where I'd started the swing shift in 1986, vendor reps—from Rockwell, Cummins Diesel, Jacobs Engine Brakes—would bring us doughnuts. To curry goodwill, they'd set out suitcase-size pink boxes packed with Bavarian crème doughnuts, jelly doughnuts, everything filled and covered with jimmies and shredded coconut. A favorite prank among my friends was to insert the nozzle of a grease gun and fill certain doughnuts with axle grease. Then to watch from behind the wire-mesh parts bins and wait for someone to bite into a doctored one. It never got old.

I'd graduated with a degree in journalism in 1986, and so many of my fellow assembly-line workers had the same degree that we used to joke that the University of Oregon School of Journalism ought to teach welding. Line workers who could weld got an extra three-dollar welding differential for every hour on the clock.

After my first book tour I'd given up any dream of escaping that factory. Two people had attended my event at the Barnes & Noble in downtown Seattle. In San Francisco, where I was driven two hours to a Barnes & Noble in Livermore, no one attended my reading. For that I'd squandered my annual week's vacation, and then it was back to Portland and Freightliner Trucks.

At 23rd Avenue Books, Bob said, "If you want to make a career out of this you'll need to bring out a new book every year. Never go longer than sixteen months without something new because after sixteen months people quit coming in that door and asking me if you have another book yet."

A book every year, I got it. The die was cast.

Bob knew his business, and being an author is nothing if not a small business. Requiring a license and...everything. The city once contacted me to request an inventory of my existing stock. I explained I was a writer, and my stock was ideas. The city asked if I had any pens or pencils on my desk. Yeah, I told them. They said I needed to count any pens and pencils lying around and file an annual report listing them as current inventory. They weren't joking. Neither am I. Neither was Bob.

"And another thing," he cautioned me, "don't use a lot of commas. People hate sentences with lots of commas. Keep your sentences short. Readers like short sentences."

Bob retired and moved to Cape Cod, he followed the Red Sox fanatically, and he died.

Twenty-Third Avenue Books closed.

Bless you, Bob Maull. May one of your many, many graves always be inside my head.

Textures

L et's get started.

Think of a story as a stream of information. At best it's an ever-changing series of rhythms. Now think of yourself, the writer, as a DJ mixing tracks.

The more music you have to sample from—the more records you have to spin—the more likely you'll keep your audience dancing. You'll have more tricks to control the mood. To calm it down to a lull. Then to raise it to a crescendo. But to always keep changing, varying, evolving the stream of information so it seems fresh and immediate and keeps the reader hooked.

If you were my student I'd want you to be aware of the many different "textures" of information at your disposal. These are best defined by the examples that follow.

When telling a story, consider mixing any or all of the following.

TEXTURES: THE THREE TYPES OF COMMUNICATION

Description: A man walks into a bar.

Instruction: Walk into a bar.

Exclamation (onomatopoeia): *Sigh.*

Most fiction consists of only description, but good story-telling can mix all three forms. For instance, "A man walks into a bar and orders a margarita. Easy enough. Mix three parts tequila and two parts triple sec with one part lime juice, pour it over ice, and—voilà—that's a margarita."

Using all three forms of communication creates a natural, conversational style. Description combined with occasional instruction, and punctuated with sound effects or exclamations: It's how people talk.

Instruction addresses the reader, breaking the fourth wall. The verbs are active and punchy. "Walk this way." Or, "Look for the red house near Ocean Avenue." And they imply useful, factual information—thus building your authority. Look at Nora Ephron's novel *Heartburn*, and how she plants recipes within the story.

In my own short story "Guts," I lapse into a long passage of instruction: "...go buy a pack of those lambskin condoms. Take one out and unroll it. Pack it with peanut butter. Smear it with petroleum jelly. Then try to tear it. Try to pull it in half." The shift from moment-to-moment description to an instructional aside creates tension because it cuts away from the action for a beat. Then, boom, we're back in the description of events.

Granted, most of what you ever write will be description, but don't hesitate to shift to instruction. Likewise, onomatopoeia shouldn't be limited to the "pow" and "blam" we see in comic books. In my novel *Pygmy*, every time I needed a mid-sentence beat of something to accentuate the end of the passage... "Trapped all day, then could be next walk to toilet, *pow-pow*, clot knock out brain." I get a greater effect at the end of the sentence by interrupting the flow with a beat of special-effects noise.

In closing, my freshman year in college, before an early-morning German course, a guy was telling a story that went, "...so we're going around this long curve—skreeeeech! vrooooom!—and we pass this police car..."

A listening girl leaned close to me and whispered, "Why do men always use sound effects in stories, but women never do?"

An excellent observation. Learn from it.

Everyone should use three types of communication. Three parts description. Two parts instruction. One part onomatopoeia. Mix to taste.

TEXTURES: MIX FIRST-, SECOND-, AND THIRD-PERSON POINTS OF VIEW

Think of a good joke. "Yesterday I walked into a bar. You know how it goes. You walk into a bar, and you expect a bartender, maybe some video poker. A man needs his distractions. No guy wants to get off work and go into some bar and see a penguin mixing drinks..."

In conversation we switch between first-, second-, and third-person points of view. The constant shift controls the intimacy and authority of our story; for instance, "I walked" has the authority of first person. Second person addresses the listeners and enlists them: "You walk." And the shift to third person controls the pace, "No guy wants," by moving from the specific "I" to the general "guy."

Arguably, first person carries the most authority because it gives us someone responsible for the story. As opposed to the third-person narration by some hidden, unknown god-like writer. Second person worked well in Jay McInerney's *Bright Lights, Big City*. It can have a hypnotic effect, but it can be tricky. Unless a story is well plotted, fast paced, and short, constant second person can annoy.

The rub is that using all three POVs means the story must ultimately be told in first person. But even second and third can be mixed to create a sense of some undeclared narrator. In *Bright Lights, Big City* the narration is second person, but every time it depicts something other than itself the narration is effectively third person.

So much of this book will be about recognizing what good storytellers do intuitively.

If you were my student, I'd tell you to shift as needed between the three POVs. Not constantly, but as appropriate to control authority, intimacy, and pace.

TEXTURES: BIG VOICE VERSUS LITTLE VOICE

You've seen this in a zillion stories. Every time Carrie Bradshaw hunches over her laptop to write her *Sex and the City* newspaper column...Every time Jane Fonda spills her guts to her psychiatrist in *Klute*...a story lapses into big voice.

The camera is little voice. The voice-over device is big voice.

Little voice (also called Recording Angel because it seems to hover and watch) depicts the moment-by-moment action. Big voice comments on it.

Little voice remains objective, giving us the smells, sounds, flavors, textures, and actions in a scene. Big voice muses.

Little voice gives us the facts. Big voice gives us the meaning—or at least a character's subjective interpretation of the events.

Not many stories exist without both voices. On *Star Trek* it's the captain's log. In *Flashdance* it's the confessional in the Catholic church. In the film *The Social Network*, the big voice expository sequences are the legal deposition scenes. At regular intervals a character is going to discuss his life with a therapist. Or she's going to write a letter or diary entry, but she's going to rise above the meat-and-potatoes reality of physical verbs. He's going to ask rhetorical questions on behalf of the reader, à la Carrie Bradshaw's "Am I the only one who's not enjoying anal sex?" Amy Adams in *Sunshine Cleaning* will use a citizens band radio to talk to her dead mother. Margaret will ask God, "Are you there?" Or Charlize Theron in *Young Adult* will lapse into the coping mechanism of writing as the teen narrator of her character's YA books.

In my own books, the device for introducing big voice is usually some nonfiction form that emerges from the character's life. In *Invisible Monsters* it's the "postcards from the future" that the characters write and discard. In *Survivor* it's the cockpit flight recorder of the doomed airliner. In *Choke* it's the Fourth Step, the written history of an addict in recovery. It begins the novel, but quickly shifts to a physical scene.

That said, consider that big voice might not be your strongest way to hook a reader at the beginning of a story. In *The Great Gatsby*, Fitzgerald devotes much of the first chapter to a rambling description of the narrator's broken heart. As does the opening monologue in *The Glass Menagerie*. Both stories have to establish that the events will take place in hindsight. They ask us to care about the narrator's regret and lost innocence. Only then do they go into flashback and specific detail to demonstrate how that heart was broken.

Yes, the Victorians loved to "put a porch" on the front of a novel. For example, "It was the best of times, it was the worst of times...yada yada." But that's a tough sell nowadays. My apologies to Nick Carraway, but few people will be hooked by a soy boy's mansplaining about his self-professed broken heart.

These days a good story is more likely to begin with a physical scene—people finding a dead body or being menaced by zombies. Little voice, not big voice. Blame this on movies. It mimics the opening "gripper" scenes in movies. As Thom Jones told me, "Action carries its own authority." The audience will engage with action. An aside: Your overseas translators will adore you for using concrete verbs. Like the action in action movies, verbs in fiction play effectively in other languages. A kiss is still a kiss. A sigh is just a sigh.

In the second scene or the second chapter, then you can risk big voice. Remember: First we see Indiana Jones rob a tomb and fight to escape past poisonous snakes and rotting corpses. Snakes, skeletons, and poison darts trigger our physical reaction. Once we're flooded with adrenaline, *then* we see him giving a boring lecture in the classroom. It's only in porn that the talky parts work better at the beginning.

Also consider that big voice might not always occur in words. Look at the stories in which a vast art project serves to comment on or clarify the main character's thoughts. In *The Day of the Locust* it's the huge mural that Todd is painting in his apartment. Called *The Burning of Los Angeles*, the work in progress depicts all the novel's characters involved in a classically inspired inferno of ridiculous architecture. Similarly, in *Close Encounters of the Third Kind*, Richard Dreyfuss externalizes his obsessive thoughts by spending much of the film sculpting a room-filling replica of the Devil's Tower in Wyoming. In the film version of my book *Choke* the past accumulates as yet another mural.

And yes, a small amount of big voice goes a long way. It works great for setting a scene. And it works great for underscoring a plot event. If you were my student I'd tell you to keep your big voice philosophizing to a minimum. Each time you shift to big voice you bump your reader out of the fictional dream, so too much commenting can slow the story's

ACTION CARRIES ITS OWN

AUTHORITY

Thom Jones

momentum to a crawl. And it can annoy by being too clever or too preachy, dictating how the reader should react.

However, switching to big voice for short stretches will allow you to imply time passing. And it can also buffer between scenes in which lots of physical action takes place. *And* it allows you to briefly summarize preceding action and deliver a witty or wise meme about life.

TEXTURES: ATTRIBUTION

By attribution I mean those little signposts inserted in dialogue that tell us who said what.

For example: "Don't make me stop this car," she said.

Or: He asked, "Who died and made you Ross Perot?"

Too often we see page-long cascades of unattributed speech. Characters exchange quips without a hint of gesture or action. Soon enough we're confused and counting backward to establish who said what.

In silent pictures actors flailed and mugged to communicate, with only an occasional line of dialogue flashed on a card. The early talking pictures became the opposite. The crude microphones required everyone to cluster in static groups near them. No one dared to move. It was years before filmmakers could combine the huge physical vocabulary of the silent era with the smart, stagy dialogue of the early sound era.

Ideally, you should be combining gesture, action, and expression with your dialogue.

First, use attribution to avoid confusing your reader. Avoid making your reader feel foolish at all costs! You want to make your reader feel smart, smarter than the main character. That way the reader will sympathize and want to root for the character. Scarlett O'Hara is charming and smart and can convince men she's beautiful. We have every reason to hate and resent her, but she's too dumb to recognize that Rhett Butler is her soul mate. So we're hooked. We feel superior and in our patronizing, condescending, voyeuristic way, we want her to smarten up. In a way, we "adopt" her.

So use attribution to avoid making your reader feel like a dummy who gets lost in long exchanges of dialogue. Better yet, I'd tell you to *never* use long exchanges of dialogue, but we'll cross that bridge when we come to it.

Second, use attribution to create a beat of…nothing. A bland, empty moment like the silence between notes in music. The theory is that readers don't subvocalize "he said." They visually leap over it, landing harder on the dialogue that follows. For example: "Nurse," he said, "hurry and get me a fresh pancreas."

Use attribution to control the delivery of dialogue, creating the sort of dramatic pause an actor would insert. Otherwise, the reader will race through a line without realizing how it ought to be weighted.

Third, use physical action as a form of attribution that also underscores or undermines what's being said. For example: "Coffee?" With her back to the room, she poured the cups full and dropped cyanide in Ellen's. "I think you'll like this new French roast."

Or: "Vampires?" Declan smirked, but his hand flew to his chest, to where he'd worn a crucifix as a child. "You're talking nonsense."

Create tension by pitting your character's gestures against his or her words. Your characters have arms and legs and faces. Use them. Use attribution. Control the delivery of dialogue. Support it with actions, or negate it with actions. Above all, do not confuse your reader by leaving it unclear who's saying what.

In closing, a reader sent me the results of a study done at the University of California, Los Angeles. People clip these things from *Scientific American* and send them to me all the time. But this one study focused on how people communicated in conversation. It found that some 83 percent of what people understood came via body language, tone of voice, and speaking volume. The actual words spoken accounted for only about 17 percent of the information passed between people.

That reminds me—my Italian editor, Eduardo, once took me to see Leonardo da Vinci's painting *The Last Supper* in Milan. You have to make a special appointment. You enter the everything-controlled room through an air lock, and get fifteen minutes to look before you're ushered out. And in that quick visit I saw how the picture is really a catalog of gesture. The body language transcends Italian or English. Honestly, all the emoticons are there in one painting.

In short, dialogue is your weakest storytelling tool.

As Tom Spanbauer always taught us, "Language is not our first language."

LANGUAGE
IS NOT
OUR FIRST
LANGUAGE

Tom Spanbauer

If you were my student, I'd make you create a list of all the quick wordless gestures you use every day. The thumbs-up. The thumb-and-index finger "okay" sign. Knocking your fist lightly on your forehead to "recall" something. Clutching your heart. The hitchhiker's thumb, which implies "get lost." The index finger held vertically against the lips for "hush up." The hooked "come here" finger. I'd make you list at least fifty hand signals. That way you'd always, always be aware of the variety of gestures you can insert into dialogue.

TEXTURES: WHAT DO YOU SAY WHEN THERE'S NOTHING TO SAY?

You've been there. You're having dinner with friends, talking up a storm. After a laugh or a sigh, the conversation falls to silence. You've exhausted a topic. The silence feels awkward, and no one puts forward a new topic. How do you tolerate that moment of nothing?

In my childhood, people filled that pause by saying, "It must be seven minutes past the hour." Superstition held that Abraham Lincoln and Jesus Christ had both died at seven minutes past the hour, so humanity would always also fall silent to honor them at that moment. I'm told that Jewish people fill that silence by saying, "A Jewish baby has been born." My point is that people have always recognized those uncomfortable moments of nothing. Their ways to bridge that silence arise from their shared history.

We need...something to hide the seam between topics. A

bland sorbet. Films can cut or dissolve or fade to. Comics simply move from panel to panel. But in prose, how do you resolve one aspect of the story and begin the next?

Of course you can move along in one unbroken moment-to-moment description, but that's so slow. Maybe too slow for the modern audience. And while people will argue that today's audience has been dumbed down by music videos and whatnot, I'd argue that today's audience is the most sophisticated that's ever existed. We've been exposed to more stories and more forms of storytelling than any people in history.

So we expect prose to move as quickly and intuitively as film. And to do this, let's consider how people do it in conversation. They "whatever." They say, "Let's agree to disagree." Or, "Other than that, Mrs. Lincoln, how did you like the play?"

My friend Ina quotes *The Simpsons* with the non sequitur, "Daffodils grow in my yard."

Whatever the saying, it acknowledges an impasse and creates the permission to introduce a new idea.

In my novel *Invisible Monsters*, it's the two sentences, "Sorry, Mom. Sorry, God." In the original short story that grew to become *Fight Club*, it's the repetition of the rules.

The goal is to create a chorus appropriate to the character. In a documentary about Andy Warhol, he said that the motto of his life had become "So what?" No matter what happened, good or bad, he could dismiss the event by thinking, *So what?* For Scarlett O'Hara it was, "I'll think about that tomorrow." In that way, a chorus is also a coping mechanism.

It hides the seams in narrative the way a strip of molding hides the junction where walls and floor meet. And it allows a person to think beyond each new drama, thus moving the story forward and allowing unresolved issues to pile up and increase tension.

If done well, it also calls up a past event. Our superstition about "seven minutes past the hour" served to reinforce our mutual identity as Christians and Americans. I'd wager that most cultures have a similar device that arises from their history.

An aside: As a kid during the dawn of television commercials for Tampax and feminine hygiene sprays I loved how one of those ads would spur my parents, grandparents, aunts, uncles, and adult cousins into lively conversation. We'd sit like dumb rocks through *Bonanza*, but the moment a douche commercial sprang up on the screen, everyone yakked like magpies to distract each other. This is a bit off-topic, but a similar phenomenon.

Among my friends in college, our coded insider talk was constant. During meals if someone had a bit of food on his chin, someone else would touch that spot on her own face and say, "You have a gazelle out of the park." On road trips, if someone needed to find a toilet, he'd say, "I have a turtle's head poking out."

My point is that these sayings reinforce our group identity. They reinforce our chosen method for coping with impasse. And they can carry the reader between shifts in prose just as easily as jump cuts carry a viewer through a film.

If you were my student I'd tell you to make a list of such

placeholders. Find them in your own life. And find them in other languages, and among people in other cultures.

Use them in your fiction. Cut fiction like film.

TEXTURES: HOW TO PASS TIME

The most basic way to imply time passing is to announce the time. Then depict some activities. Then give the time. Boring stuff. Another way is to list the activities, giving lots of details, task after task, and to suddenly arrive at the streetlights blinking on or a chorus of mothers calling their kids to dinner. And these methods are fine, if you want to risk losing your reader's interest. Besides, in Minimalist writing abstract measurements such as two o'clock or midnight are frowned upon for reasons we'll discuss in the section on Establishing Your Authority.

As a better option, consider the montage. Think of a chapter or passage that ticks off the cities of a road trip, giving a quirky detail about what happened in each. It's just city, city, city, like the compressed European tour montage near the end of Bret Ellis's *Rules of Attraction*. Or picture the little cartoon airplane we see navigate the globe from city to city in old movies, quickly delivering us to Istanbul.

In Tama Janowitz's *Slaves of New York*, the montage is a list of the daily menus in an asylum. Monday we eat this. Tuesday, this. Wednesday, this. In the Bob Fosse film *All That Jazz* it's the repeated, every-morning quick-cut sequence of the main character brushing his teeth and taking Benzedrine and telling the bathroom mirror, "It's showtime!"

Whether you depict cities or meals or boyfriends, keep them brief and compress them together. When the montage ends we'll arrive at an actual scene, but with the sense that considerable time has passed.

Another method to imply time passing is intercutting. End one scene and jump to a flashback, alternating between the past and present. That way, when you jump back to the present you won't have to arrive at the moment you left off. Each jump allows you to fudge time, implying it's passed.

Or you can intercut between characters. Think of the various plot threads in John Berendt's *Midnight in the Garden of Good and Evil* or in Armistead Maupin's *Tales of the City*. As each character meets an obstacle, we jump to a different character. It's maddening if the reader is invested in just one character, but every jump moves us forward in time.

Or cut between big voice and little voice. With this in mind, think of the varied chapters in Steinbeck's *The Grapes of Wrath*. At times we're with the Joad family as little-voice narration depicts them on their journey. Other times we're reading a big-voice passage that looks down in a generalized way to comment about the drought, the stream of displaced migrants, or the wary landowners and lawmen in California. Then we cut back to the Joads farther along their route. Then we cut to a big-voice chapter about the weather and the rising floods. Then we cut back to the family.

If you were my student I'd hem and haw but eventually tell you about using the space break to imply time passing. You just end a scene or passage and allow a wide margin of blank page before you begin a new scene. I'm told that early pulp novels used no chapter breaks. They just used smaller space breaks so publishers could avoid the blank page or page and a half that might be wasted between chapters. This saved a few pages of newsprint in each book, and that helped the profit margin.

In my novel *Beautiful You* I used space breaks instead of chapter breaks because I wanted to mimic the appearance of mass-market pornographic paperback books. In *1984* Orwell mentions pornographic novels written by machine for the proletariat—that and the raunchy, absurd genre of "Slash" fiction inspired me to mimic their use of white space for transitions.

The writer Monica Drake tells of studying under Joy Williams in the MFA program at the University of Arizona. Williams scanned a story submitted to the workshop and sighed, "Ah, white space…the writer's false friend."

Perhaps it's because a space break—without cutting to something different, a different time period or character or voice—can allow the writer to revisit the same elements without creating tension. For example, if we use space breaks to cut between the events in Robert's day, the story could get monotonous. But if we cut back and forth between Robert and Cynthia and some ancestor of them both in Renaissance Venice, the reader gets time away from each element and can better appreciate it and worry about outcomes.

So if you were my student I'd allow you to start out using space breaks to imply the passage of time. But don't get comfortable. Those training wheels are going to come off sooner rather than later.

TEXTURES: LISTS

To add a new texture to any story never hesitate to insert a list. Look at the guest list inserted so beautifully at the beginning of chapter 4 in *The Great Gatsby*. Bret Easton Ellis once told me that Fitzgerald's list inspired the guest list in *Glamorama*. Also look at Tim O'Brien's lists in *The Things They Carried*. A favorite is chapter 18 from Nathanael West's *The Day of the Locust*. There the main character pursues a girl through the standing sets of a Hollywood movie studio of the 1920s. Strung together are fake monuments and antiquities, every culture and time period in history crammed cheek-to-jowl, the modern world juxtaposed with dinosaurs. It might be the most perfectly surreal passage in all literature.

If you were my student I'd tell you to read it, chapter 18, then to read the sequence in Fitzgerald's *The Last Tycoon* where an earthquake causes a flood at a similar Hollywood studio and the main character looks on as a long parade of fake monuments and antiquities goes floating past. Note how West has us moving through his litany of objects while Fitzgerald fixes us in one place as the objects move.

Lists break up the page, visually. They force the reader to really read word by word. I loved listing the colors of Ikea furniture in *Fight Club*, and my dream for *Adjustment Day* was to write a book of lists that all supported a mythic, unseen list of people to be assassinated.

So, lists. Use them.

TEXTURES: DEPICT A SOCIAL MODEL
THROUGH REPETITION

Do you remember how, as a child, you could throw some boards on the ground and dictate a new reality? "The dirt is lava. The boards are the only safe way across." Kids can instantly imagine a new setting. They make up the rules. The world becomes what they mutually agree it will be. The tree is safe. The sidewalk is enemy territory.

If you were my student I'd tell you a secret that Barry Hannah told me: "Readers love that shit."

Just look at the successful novels that dictate how people should behave in a group. Novels like *How to Make an American Quilt* and *The Divine Secrets of the Ya-Ya Sisterhood* and *The Joy Luck Club*. These are groups bound by the rules and rituals they've agreed upon. *The Sisterhood of the Traveling Pants* is another of the many books that model a way for women to come together and share their stories. For men, there are fewer examples. The only ones that come to mind are *The Dead Poets Society* and, of course, *Fight Club*.

My guess is that people haven't a clue how to get along. They need a structure, rules, and roles to play. Once those are established, people can gather and compare their lives. They can learn from each other.

Tom Spanbauer always said, "Writers write because they weren't invited to a party." So bear in mind that the reader is also alone. A reader is more likely to feel socially awkward and crave a story that offers a way to be in the company

Barry Hannah

of others. The reader, alone in bed or alone in an airport crowded with strangers, will respond to the party scenes at Jay Gatsby's mansion.

That's the reason so many of my books depict a social model, be it the Party Crashing game in *Rant* or tightly structured movie-set protocol in *Snuff*. Once you establish your rules and begin to repeat them, they provide the framework in which characters can feel confident. The characters know how to behave. And they'll begin to relax and reveal themselves.

It was years before I understood why I wrote these social model books. It wasn't until I'd been introduced to the work of the cultural anthropologist Victor Turner. He suggests that people create "liminoid" events as a kind of social experiment. Each is a short-lived society in which people agree to be equals. Communitas, he called it. If the experiment is a success: if it serves people by providing community, fun, stress relief, self-expression, whatever…then it gradually becomes an institution. The best recent example is Burning Man, the festival in the Black Rock Desert of Nevada. Another example is Santa Rampage, the gatherings of revelers all dressed as Santa Claus and all going by the name Santa Claus. Both have passed from being spontaneous fringe happenings to becoming beloved traditions.

It's possible no one is as lonely as writers. Experts have made the case that Ken Kesey based the lunatics in *One Flew Over the Cuckoo's Nest* on the workshop he attended at Stanford. Likewise, Toni Morrison most likely based the plantation in *Beloved* on her own writing workshop, and

Robert Olen Butler based the bus passengers in his novel *Mr. Spaceman* on his writing workshop.

The linguistic anthropologist Shirley Brice Heath has said that a book will only become a classic if it binds together a community of readers. So recognize that reading is a lonely pastime. Don't shy away from inventing rituals in your story. Invent rules and prayers. Give people roles to play and lines to recite. Include some form of communion and confession, a way for people to tell their stories and find connection with others.

To heighten this ritual effect, consider creating a "template" chapter. Using one existing chapter, change minor details and make it arrive at a fresh epiphany. Chances are the reader won't realize what you've done, but will unconsciously recognize the repeated structure. Use this template to create three chapters placed equal distances apart in the book.

In this world where so many fraternal organizations and religions are disappearing, if you were my student I'd tell you to use ritual and repetition to invent new ones for your readers. Give people a model they can replicate and characters to emulate.

TEXTURES: PARAPHRASING VERSUS QUOTING

Consider that when you put a character's dialogue in quotes you give the character greater reality. Conversely when you paraphrase someone you distance and diminish them.

For example, paraphrased dialogue: I told them to put the box in the corner.

Versus: I told them, "Put the box in the corner."

In *Fight Club* I chose to put everyone's dialogue in quotes—except for the narrator's. Even Tyler occurs as more real because his words are quoted. So whenever you want to undermine what's being said, paraphrase it. If you want to negate or lessen a character, paraphrase what they say.

When you want to showcase a character, put their dialogue in quotation marks. Include attribution. Underscore the speech with a gesture.

It's a subtle effect, but if you were my student I'd tell you it works.

A Postcard from the Tour

Kim Ricketts told me the Stephen King story. We'd gone to Belltown after an event at the University of Washington bookstore. Over beers, she told me she was branching out, beginning to plan speaker events for corporations like Microsoft and Starbucks. I needed a ride back to my hotel, but Kim was smart and funny, and before the Stephen King story she told me the Al Franken story, which is why the University of Washington now required people attending an author appearance to actually buy the book. Because Al Franken had filled all eight-hundred-plus seats in Kane Hall, and the students had laughed at everything Franken had said. Attendance cost the audience members nothing, but by the end of the night Franken had sold a whopping eight books.

As per the new policy, book purchase would henceforth be required.

To snag a Stephen King event, Kim said she'd had to agree

to his standard terms. She'd had to hire bodyguards and find a venue that would hold five thousand people. Each person could bring three items to have autographed by Mr. King. The event would last some eight hours, and someone would have to stand beside the signing table and hold an ice pack to the author's shoulder for the duration.

The day arrived, and Kim held the ice pack to the shoulder in question. The venue, Town Hall, a deconsecrated church on Capitol Hill, has a jaw-dropping view of downtown Seattle. It was filled with the five thousand mostly young people, all ready to wait hours for their three signatures.

King sat and began to sign autographs. Kim stood holding the ice pack to his pesky shoulder. Not a hundred books into the eventual fifteen thousand, Kim said that King looked up at her and asked, "Can you get me some bandages?"

He showed her his signing hand, how the skin along the thumb and index finger had fossilized into a thick callus from a lifetime of marathon book signings. These calluses are the writer's equivalent of a wrestler's cauliflower ear. Thick as the armor on the hide of a stegosaurus, the calluses had begun to crack.

"I'm bleeding on the stock," King said. He showed fresh blood smudged on his pen and a partial fingerprint of blood on the title page of a book belonging to a waiting young man who didn't appear the least bit distressed to see his property stained by the vital fluids of the great wordsmith and teller of tales.

Kim started to step away, but it was too late. The next person in line had overheard the exchange and shouted, "No fair!" He shouted, "If Mr. King bleeds in his books then he has to bleed in mine!"

This, everyone in the building heard. Shrieks of indignation filled the cavernous hall as five thousand horror fans each demanded their own ration of celebrity blood. Echoes of rage boomed off the vaulted ceiling. Kim could scarcely hear as King asked, "Can you help me out?"

Still pressing the ice pack against him, she said, "They're your readers...I'll do what you decide."

King went back to signing. Signing and bleeding. Kim stayed beside him, and as the crowd saw that no bandages were forthcoming, the protest gradually subsided. Five thousand people. Each with three items. Kim told me that it took eight hours, but King managed to sign his name and smear a trace of his blood in every book. By the end of the event he was so weak the bodyguards had to carry him under the armpits to his Lincoln Town Car.

Even then, as the car pulled out to deliver him to his hotel, the disaster wasn't over.

A group of people who'd been shut out of the event because of overcrowding jumped into their own car and chased King's. These book lovers rammed and totaled the Lincoln—all for the opportunity to meet their favorite author.

In that tavern, Kim and I sat looking out the window at the empty street. Pondering the night.

Her dream had been to open a bookstore in Seattle's Ballard neighborhood, a store that sold only cookbooks. She'd die of amyloidosis in 2011. Kim Ricketts's dream bookstore, Book Larder, is still open.

But that night it was just Kim and me in an otherwise deserted bar. A little drunk, but not much. Shaking my head over her Stephen King story, I asked, "So that's the big fame we're all striving for?"

Kim sighed. "Them's be the big leagues."

Bless you, Kim Ricketts. May one of your many, many graves always be inside my head.

Establishing Your Authority

E stablish your authority," Tom Spanbauer used to tell us, "and you can do anything." As his students we made lapel buttons printed with this dictum and wore them the way members of a religion would wear crucifixes and the like. It was our creed. A part of the Ten Commandments of Minimalism: Don't use Latinate words. Don't use abstracts. Don't use received text...And once you establish your authority, you can do anything.

To that I'd add the Thom Jones advice: Action carries its own authority. If you move through each scene with clear, physical verbs—taking steps, touching objects—your reader's mind will follow as closely as a dog's eyes track a squirrel.

If you were my student I'd ask you to consider the following methods for building authority within a story. Make the reader believe you. Make the incredible seem inevitable.

AUTHORITY: THE AUTHORITY SPEECH

You've seen the typical authority speech given in many movies. In *My Cousin Vinny* it's near the end of the courtroom trial when Marisa Tomei seizes the moment and gives her passionate lecture about the 1955 Chevrolet Bel Air with a 327-cubic-inch engine and a four-barrel carburetor.

In *The Devil Wears Prada* it's the recent history of the color cerulean blue used in fashion, a speech delivered in minute detail by Meryl Streep as she assembles clothing for a model.

The film *Legally Blonde* contains two such speeches. The first occurs in a Rodeo Drive clothing store, where Reese Witherspoon upbraids a salesclerk by delivering a boatload of facts that expose the clerk as a liar. The second speech occurs late in the trial sequence when Witherspoon lectures on the chemistry of permanent waves, using facts that decimate the testimony of a prosecution witness.

For quick, powerful proof of a character's authority, few tactics work as well as allowing her to reel off facts that demonstrate she boasts a depth of technical knowledge no one would've expected. Recent politics make this a device useful for female characters, but not so useful for males. First because there has to be an expectation that the character is vapid. The surprise comes when a seemingly dim-witted character demonstrates a deep understanding of something crucial. Consider the dream sequence in *Romy and Michele's High School Reunion* where Lisa Kudrow recites the process for making glue. And alas, the airhead character is more likely to be a female.

These days such a speech delivered by a male character would come across as tedious mansplaining, at best. At worst, as Asperger's syndrome. Still, there are male examples. Just watch *Good Will Hunting* for the scenes where Matt Damon spouts erudition to dominate would-be geniuses in university taverns.

Another aside: Wes, the editor in the background—always there, never noticed—suggests that an authority speech makes a character more likable. I find the whole concept of "likability" to be problematic. We'll revisit this, but I'd rather respect a character. Frankly I don't even like likable people.

So if you were my student, and you needed to give a character authority—and build your own as the author—introduce the character as simple-minded, then have her or him let rip with a string of esoteric, complicated facts that shock the audience.

AUTHORITY: THE DEAD PARENT

Scratch the surface of any comedy and you'll find a dead mother or father. It's the unresolved, irresolvable hurt that generates all the wisecracking and antics.

Even in dramas, it's the background tragedy that makes the foreground dramas bearable.

The dead relative is everywhere.

In the Earl Hamner television series *The Waltons*, it's John

Walton's dead brother, killed in World War I, the never-mentioned ghost that the young Ben Walton is named for. In *The Big Valley* the patriarch, Tom Barkley, has died, leaving Barbara Stanwyck to run the ranch. In *Bonanza* the matriarch is dead. In *Julia*, starring Diahann Carroll, the patriarch has died flying a helicopter in Vietnam. In *The Courtship of Eddie's Father* the mother is dead. In *The Ghost and Mrs. Muir* the father is dead. In *Nanny and the Professor* the mother is dead. In *Ellery Queen*, mother dead.

Among hit comedies, the body count is staggering. *The Andy Griffith Show*, mother dead. *The Beverly Hillbillies*, mother dead. *My Three Sons*, dead mother. *One Day at a Time*, dead father. *Alice*, dead father. *Phyllis*, dead father. *The Partridge Family*, dead father. *Family Affair*, both parents dead. *The Brady Bunch*, two parents dead. *Party of Five*, parents dead.

If you were my student I'd ask: "Why is it that so many successful plots begin at the family plot?"

Because for most of us—especially among young people—our worst fear is of losing our parents. If you create a world where one or both parents have died, you're creating characters that have survived your reader's worst fears. Your reader will respect them from the get-go. Even though the surviving offspring might be children or teenagers, their unspoken pain and loss will cast them as adults in the reader's mind.

Plus, from the first page, anything that happens will be survivable because the characters have already survived the worst. A dead parent bonds the surviving family in ways your reader would like to be bonded with his or her family.

To create a story in which the reader never thinks to criticize the characters, kill the mother or father before the first page.

AUTHORITY: GET THE SMALL STUFF RIGHT

Someone once told me a secret about the stained-glass windows in cathedrals. He began by telling me how these windows served to teach scripture to the illiterate. They were the dazzling CinemaScope Cecil B. DeMille epics of their time. The summer blockbusters, these towering depictions of Jonah inside the whale, the parting of the Red Sea, the Ascension of Christ.

The trick to making a miracle believable was to place it high in the window, far from the lowly viewer. All the truly meticulous work went into creating the details people would see first, along the lower edge.

If the viewers could believe the details at their own level — the plants on the ground, the sandals, the folds in the hem of a garment — they would believe the miracle depicted higher up in the window. Manna could fall from Heaven. Halos could hover above heads and angels could fly among the clouds.

During the filming of *Fight Club*, I asked director David Fincher if the audience would accept the ultimate reveal that Brad Pitt's character was imaginary. Fincher's response was, "If they believe everything up to that point, they'll believe the plot twist."

With that in mind, if you were my student I'd tell you

to focus on breaking down a gesture and describing it so effectively that the reader unconsciously mimics it. Not everything, but the crucial objects and actions should be unpacked. In Shirley Jackson's story "The Lottery," note how she lingers on the box from which the papers are drawn. She describes where it's stored, how it was crafted, what it replaced. All of this attention lavished on a plain wooden box helps us accept the horrible purpose for it. If we believe in the box, we'll believe the ritual murder it facilitates.

Get the smallest item wrong at your own peril...On tour for my book *Beautiful You* I met a young woman who said I consistently botched the details of my young female protagonist. I asked her to give an example, to tell me the most unrealistic quality I'd given Penny Harrigan—a girl from Nebraska who masturbates with the mummified finger of her dead sex coach and is erotically tormented by remote-controlled tiny robots implanted in her by the world's richest man who seeks to genetically reengineer his long-dead wife...

"Your most unrealistic detail about Penny?" asked the reader.

Yes, I wanted to know the biggest thing I'd gotten wrong.

She thought for a moment. "That's easy. You say her favorite ice cream is butter brickle." She shook her head at my stupidity. "That's an old-man flavor."

I asked what Penny's favorite flavor should've been.

"Chocolate," she said. "Anything chocolate."

Case closed. The smallest mistake can destroy all believability.

AUTHORITY: THE AUTHORITY OF TRUISMS

The job of the creative person is to recognize and express things for others. Some haven't fully grasped their own feelings. Others lack the skill to communicate the feeling or idea. Still others lack the courage to express it.

Whatever the case, we recognize the truth when we read it. The best writers seem to read our minds, and they nail exactly what we've never been able to put into words.

In her novel *Heartburn*, Nora Ephron wrote, "When you're single you date other singles. And when you're a couple you date other couples." Reading those words, I was willing to believe anything she put on the page after that.

The same goes for Amy Hempel, who wrote, "What dogs want is for no one to ever leave."

Fran Lebowitz once wrote, "The opposite of talking isn't listening. The opposite of talking is waiting."

Armistead Maupin invented Mona's Law. It states that of a great lover, a great job, and a great apartment, in life you can have one. At most you can have two of the three. But you will never, ever have all three at the same time.

Truman Capote wrote, "You can tell what a man really thinks of you by the earrings he gives you."

Such a well-worded aphorism carries all the authority of Confucius or Oscar Wilde. A wise, intuitive observation can convey more power than all the facts in Wikipedia.

WHAT DOGS WANT IS FOR NO ONE TO EVER LEAVE

Amy Hempel

AUTHORITY: YOUR STORYTELLING CONTEXT

In our world of fake news…this world in which the internet has eroded the credibility of all information…people want to know the context of a story just as much as they want to hear the story itself. Context and source are more important now than they've ever been.

So if you were my student, I'd ask you, "Who's telling this? Where are they telling it? And why are they telling it?"

Look around. The world is filled with forums in which people tell their stories. These are gold mines where writers can find material. They're also great settings in which to frame stories. While researching my books *Choke* and *Invisible Monsters*, I loved to call telephone sex chat lines. Here was channel after channel of people telling their stories. If one got boring, I'd just transfer to another. And if a story maybe wasn't plotted so well I'd listen for the verbal tricks and tics that reinforced its truth. Rainy afternoons, I'd sit and jot notes holding the phone to my ear. These spoken anecdotes were wonderful and raw, and I'd look for similar patterns or themes that might allow me to cobble several together into a short story or a series of scenes. Who knows, someday I might set a story in the context of a 976 sex hotline. It would be especially poignant to hear a tragic story told over a tawdry phone sex line. Or even better, to hear a tale of redemption in the low-culture context of people talking dirty talk.

Another context for storytelling is addiction recovery groups. They really do serve as the new churches where people go to confess their worst selves and to be accepted back by their communities. Even if the stories are lackluster, they're told by people who have years of practice. Outside of stand-up comedy, there's not much oral storytelling left in America. But it's thriving in 12-step support groups. Stand-up comedy versus sit-down tragedy. It goes without saying that no one's confidence should be betrayed—but you can learn effective storytelling tactics. Better skills—for free and with free coffee—than you can learn in many MFA programs. And what about a story in which someone *does* steal a story from Alcoholics Anonymous and turns it into a hugely successful movie…? Imagine the rage, envy, revenge that act would engender while still keeping the reader's sympathy.

Another excellent storytelling context is late-night radio. All that talk about Bigfoot, black helicopters, restless ghosts, Martians…it serves as a bedtime story for adults. The strange and fantastic plumbs the subconscious like a fairy tale does. The radio's voice evokes dreamlike images that guide us into our nightmares. Listeners call and contribute their own anecdotes that support the general theme of the evening. It's Scheherazade telling her endless stories in the *Arabian Nights*.

Yet another albeit unlikely context for stories is any of the cable television shopping channels. Any product will do, but my preference is for the jewelry channels where goofy folks with relatable down-home accents offer up pearl necklaces while spinning yarns about how your friends and family will admire and envy you for owning such a necklace. It's like a guided meditation. "Just picture how the ladies at your church will flock to ooh and aah over this emerald ring! Why, you'll be the center of attention. Everyone will turn green with jealousy!" And if status doesn't hook you, they pitch you with love. "Your baby granddaughter will treasure this pinkie ring for the rest of her life, and every time she wears it she'll remember you..."

So if you were my student I'd task you with writing a story in the persona of a customer phoning the channel and telling a story related to a recent purchase.

One great aspect of choosing an existing storytelling context is that the context dictates the structure and transitions. A phone sex hotline implies the ever-present ticking clock of credit card charges. The radio show includes commercial breaks. All of your framing devices are there and need no invention.

As a final example of a context, here's a favorite. Some of the toughest men I know, former fire jumpers, active military, they love those antiques appraisal shows. *Antiques Roadshow* on public television, in particular. People bring in family heirlooms, and an expert examines the items. The owner tells the item's history, usually linked to the family's ancestry. And the expert either confirms or denies that story. Often the owner is publically devastated to find his dead relations were fools or liars. The item is not what it has always been supposed to be. Sometimes the item is appraised at a small fortune, but often it's dismissed as junk.

In one quick public ritual, we're presented with an emotionally fraught saga and the object that supports it. In the next moment the saga is disproved. The family's idea of itself is dealt a serious blow, and all of this takes place on camera. The constant threat of ritual humiliation is why tough men love this show. The mighty are brought low. The prideful, shamed.

Even if the antique in question proves to be authentic and worth big money, there's still a loss. All of its epic, magical power, the heroic tale of Great-Uncle Who's It charging into battle with this sword or whatnot held high…it's still reduced to a dollars-and-cents amount. Its power now limited by what the market will pay for it.

It's the *Ye Olde Curiosity Shoppe*–type anthology, updated.

Now if I were your teacher, I'd tell you to write a story in which a jaded on-air appraiser is asked to confirm the value of a cursed monkey's paw…a shrunken head…the Holy Grail.

AUTHORITY: CRIBBING AUTHENTICITY FROM A NONFICTION FORM

Among the easiest ways to establish your authority is to steal it. Think of Orson Welles's radio broadcast of H. G. Wells's *The War of the Worlds*. By adopting all the conventions of nonfiction newscasts, Welles made a ludicrous story so believable that millions of people panicked. They fled their homes. They called their loved ones and bid them goodbye.

Think of the film *The Blair Witch Project*. Simply by saying that the story consists of documentary footage recovered after a team of investigators went missing, the film was able to rise above its rough edges and to frighten people. Likewise, the film *Fargo* risked being another slapstick crime caper like *Raising Arizona* until the Coen Brothers thought to add a single card statement on the front. A somber black screen with white lettering claims the story was based on actual events (it's not).

Think of *Citizen Kane*, which used the device of a newsreel to summarize the plot at the start of the film, then used faceless journalists to tie together the subsequent scenes. The interviews become the device for transitioning between different points of view and time periods. And all the while, the fact that they're "reporters" injects the melodramatic story with a gravity and reality that sells it to the audience.

Nonfiction forms have shaped our most famous authors. Hemingway's first writing job was as a reporter covering the crime beat on the *Kansas City Star*. He took to heart the paper's in-house style guide, which demanded short, choppy sentences filled with active verbs. And for the rest of his career he wrote terse prose based on that same highly readable newspaper style. Likewise, Fitzgerald's first writing job was to crank out advertisement copy. Forever after, his fiction was filled with images of advertising, brand names, and the seductive lyrical sentences that still charm us.

So if you were my student I'd tell you that a nonfiction form will allow you to make even the most fantastic, the most maudlin, the most silly story seem completely plausible.

In so many of my own novels I've used nonfiction forms. In *Choke* the form is the fourth step of the 12-step recovery program, a written summation of the addict's life. In *Rant* it's the form of an oral history, numerous interviews intercut to tell the story of someone now absent. Among my models for that book was Jean Stein's *Edie: An American Biography*, the story of Edith Sedgwick. And much of the structure of my *Invisible Monsters* was based on the chaotic layout of the fashion magazines I'd see at the laundromat where I washed my clothes each week.

Besides lending fiction a greater sense of reality, a non-fiction form dictates the structure of the work and the ways to transition between scenes. In fashion magazines, for instance, articles simply "jump" to a designated page elsewhere in the issue. In oral histories each new speaker is designated by his name and a colon placed before his statement.

My *Pygmy* appears to be a series of "dispatches" sent by a spy reporting on his progress during a secret mission. It was Chelsea Cain, in workshop, who suggested that I used black blocks to occlude certain details and make the "document" seem redacted. The effect worked so well I wished I'd used it more. Consequently I did, by placing "real" rose petals and pills on the pages of *Fight Club 2*, to hide characters' faces and thereby undermine the sincerity of what they might say. Or to hide their dialogue and negate its cleverness. Thank you, Chelsea.

Any aspect of the nonfiction form that seems like an innate flaw—the jerky camerawork in *Cloverfield* and over-the-top acting—becomes an asset when you mimic it while using that form for fiction. The graininess of black-and-white security cameras, for instance, adds another texture and a fresh point of view to conventional film. In the film *Fight Club* director

David Fincher cuts to such footage for an "objective" perspective that shows the narrator fighting himself.

So if I were your teacher, I'd tell you to study how each nonfiction form isn't perfect. Find its flaws and use those to make your fiction seem more real and less polished and writerly.

AUTHORITY: FORGET BEING LIKABLE

Welcome to America, our never-ending, great popularity contest. And to capitalism, where likability trumps everything else.

If you were my student, I'd tell you to forget about being liked. Tastes change over time, public taste as well as personal taste. Your work might not be immediately celebrated, but if it remains lodged in someone's memory you have a good chance of being embraced over time. The first time I read the books foisted on me in college—*Jane Eyre*, *One Flew Over the Cuckoo's Nest*, *The Caucasian Chalk Circle*—I hated them. But over time I've gone back to reread them, and they've become my favorites.

Witness the movies that premiered to damning reviews. *The Night of the Living Dead. Harold and Maude. Blade Runner.* They found a place in public memory, and time has made them classics. So do not write to be liked. Write to be remembered.

AUTHORITY: WRITE FROM WITHIN
THE POINT OF VIEW

This next skill might be the most difficult part of writing you'll ever tackle. But once you get the knack of it, it will make writing easier and more fun than you ever could've imagined.

Instead of writing about a character, write from within the character.

This means that every way the character describes the world must describe the character's experience. You and I never walk into the same room as each other. We each see the room through the lens of our own life. A plumber enters a very different room than a painter enters.

This means you can't use abstract measurements. No more six-foot-tall men. Instead you must describe a man's size based on how your character or narrator perceives a man whose height is seventy-two inches. A character might say "a man too tall to kiss" or "a man her dad's size when he's kneeling in church." You may not describe the temperature as being one hundred degrees. Or trips as being fifty miles long. All standardized measurements preclude you describing how your character sees the world.

So no more five-year-old girls. No more seven o'clock. No two-ton trucks.

Yes, it's a pain, having to break down the details and translate them through a character's point of view. But only at first. With a little practice you'll begin to see the world via the character's experience and the descriptions will come naturally.

Eventually, it will even be fun.

Getting inside a character might seem like a vacation from being you. But face it, you're never not you. No matter what world you create you're always dealing with your own shit. Same shit, different mask. You've chosen to explore a certain character because something about it resonates with you. Don't pretend for a moment that writing as a different person is evading reality. If anything it allows you a greater freedom to explore parts of yourself you wouldn't dare consciously examine.

Another part of writing from within a character is using language as only that character would. No two people speak the same. Each has her own little wardrobe of phrases and slang. Each misuses words differently. For instance, I've noticed that people from larger families always use a clause to seize attention before they say anything.

They'll say, "Get this. It's going to freeze tonight."

Short aside: While researching for my book *Rant* I attended a seminar for used car salespeople. In it the instructor explained that people are usually one of three types: the visual, the auditory, or the tactile. The visual will preface each statement with visual terms. "Look here..." or "I see, but..." The auditory will use terms based on hearing: "Listen up..." or "I hear what you're saying." The tactile will use physical, active terms: "I catch your drift," or, "I can't wrap my mind around it." Bullshit or not, it's a good place to start. Which way will your character skew?

More important, what consistent language mistakes will he or she make?

According to Tom Spanbauer, his teacher Gordon Lish called this calculated flawed language "burnt tongue." Lish advocated that stories should not sound as if they've been written by a writer. Stories have greater authority if they're delivered with the same passion and flawed language that an actual person would use telling the emotion-laden truth.

So if writing from within a character, you should "burn" the language. Customize it to the speaker. Even when writing in third person, make the language reflect the character's perspective and experience.

To all of Spanbauer's and Lish's advice, I'd just add: Make language your bitch.

Create a pidgin language for your character. Look how successfully it works in David Sedaris's collection *Me Talk Pretty One Day*. Or in my own novel *Pygmy* and my short story "Eleanor." Not to mention Irvine Welsh's *Trainspotting*. Readers have so many ways of determining meaning in a sentence. They look at context as well as words. So it's a great trick to subvert reader expectation by writing a long, elegant passage that ends flatly on exactly the wrong word.

Early in the publishing process an editor told me that most successful copy editors learned English as a second language. They studied scrupulously what most Americans learned haphazardly. The result is that they know exactly where to place every comma, and how to use a semicolon, and they're trained to iron out the mis-phrasings that keep narrative voice fresh and authentic.

The idiot character is more fun to hear because he bends the language for his purpose. So does the ESL character or the child. When we read *The Color Purple* the language demonstrates the narrator's innocence from the book's first word. This instantly primes us to care for and root for the character.

Beyond that, no abstracts (no inches, miles, minutes, days, decibels, tons, lumens) because the way someone depicts the world should more accurately depict him. Unless, of course, you're depicting a scientist who scores high on the autism spectrum.

And no perfect newscaster language because the story should not sound fake, as if written by a writer.

Lastly, avoid what Spanbauer and Lish call "received text." Meaning, no clichés.

AUTHORITY: PLAY TO THE STRENGTH OF YOUR MEDIUM

The pros: Books are cheap to write. They cost little more than time. And they're cheap to produce and distribute, especially compared with films, which require huge consensus to come together. Books require a certain level of intelligence to consume so they're less likely to fall into the wrong hands: a child's, for example. Thus books can tackle topics not suited for children, whereas films can be so easily consumed that they must always self-censor.

Books are also consumed in private. In most cases this means one person making the continued effort to read and thereby giving her ongoing consent. Contrast this with films, which might be shown on airplanes to both consenting and nonconsenting viewers. Films cost a relative fortune to create and therefore must be presentable on television to make a profit. Comics…comics and graphic novels can offer almost the spectacle of film, without the music. But their ease of consumption means they must self-censor.

The cons: Books take an enormous amount of time and energy to consume, compared with films. Prose can't convey the spectacle that film can. Most books fail to viscerally engage the audience. They might act upon your mind and emotions, but they seldom generate a sympathetic physical reaction. Compared with video games, books offer no way for the audience to actively control events. But video games are less likely to explore the full spectrum of emotion and ultimately break the audience's heart.

An aside: Among the strengths of film is its ability to depict motion. And as always action carries its own authority. Consider how many "movies" include crucial scenes that are resolved by a spectacular dance. Among them are *Napoleon Dynamite*, *Pee-wee's Big Adventure* (the tequila dance atop the bar), *Romy and Michele's High School Reunion*, *Flashdance*, *Footloose*, *Saturday Night Fever*…In contrast, duh, dance sequences are less effective in novels.

So when choosing an idea for a book, make sure it's an idea that only a book can best present. If it's an idea that film, comics, or gaming can depict, why bother writing the book?

If you were my student I'd tell you to write the most

outlandish, challenging, provocative stories. Take full advantage of the complete freedom books provide. To not take advantage of that freedom is to waste the one chief strength of the medium.

AUTHORITY: HOW DO YOU GET TO IMPOSSIBLE?

How do you convince a reader of something beyond his own experience?

You start with what he does know, and you move in baby steps toward what he doesn't. One of my favorite examples of this comes from the novel *The Contortionist's Handbook* by Craig Clevenger. To paraphrase, he tells the reader to imagine waking up on a Monday morning filled with dread. Another stultifying week looms. Another soul-crushing day at work, doing something you'd never planned to do for the rest of your life. You're growing older, your life wasted, your dreams lost. And then you realize it's actually Sunday morning. That rush of relief...that flood of joy and bliss that fills you and buoys your whole body with euphoria, multiply that feeling by ten, and that's how a Vicodin feels.

Bravo, Clevenger. He takes a sensation we've all felt and uses it as a bridge to understand something we might not have experienced. He effectively communicates the physical effects of a painkilling drug.

That's using what I call "cultural precedent" and moving the reader from a common experience, through several intermediary, escalating examples, and ultimately arriving at an extreme the reader could've and would've never accepted if you'd presented it from the start.

I love this form. In arguably my most successful short story, "Guts," I tell a series of increasingly funny and unsettling anecdotes about failed experiments in masturbation. The first gets laughs. The second anecdote gets laughs but ends badly. The third gets a lot of laughs, so much laughter that I'm forced to stop reading aloud until the laughter subsides, but by then the audience has been charmed beyond the point of no return. That third anecdote takes a sudden turn and barrels full-speed into horror. If the audience had any idea where the story would end, they would've walked out at the beginning.

Likewise, with my story "The Toad Prince" (originally titled "The Garden of Ethan" for obvious reasons), I move the reader through more and more extreme-yet-common examples of body modification. Each creates more dread until the final extended reveal.

It's a useful structure, stringing anecdotes together to illustrate a theme. And it gradually walks the reader from the believable to the incredible.

Also consider how past stories create a precedent for new versions. Among my favorites is the "burning animal" story. One example is the story "Strays" by Mark Richard. Another is the anecdote about the burning mouse in David Sedaris's *When You Are Engulfed in Flames*. On a book tour, as a publicist in Los Angles was driving me to the Skirball Center, she pointed out a house we were passing in the Hollywood

Hills. She explained that friends had bought the house and couldn't understand why it stank during cold weather. It jutted from a steep slope. Floor-to-ceiling windows seemed to hold up the flat roof. She said that the living room featured a gas fireplace where blue flames danced on an open bed of crushed white granite.

As the neighbors eventually revealed, the previous owners had a cat. The cat had always used the crushed granite as a litter box, and each time the fireplace was turned on it became a stinking barbecue of broiling cat shit.

I told that story to a publicist in Seattle, on the same tour, and she told me an almost identical version. Friends of hers had actually come home late one night and switched on the heat. Something, some screaming banshee demon, had exploded from the fireplace and set fire to the living room curtains. Their cat, it turned out to be.

There it was as perfectly formed as myth: A new example of the burning animal story. Horrible and sad, but acceptable because existing cultural precedent made it familiar to the reader.

If you were my student I'd tell you to read the story "The Enormous Radio" by John Cheever. Then read "Call Guy" by Alec Wilkinson in *The New Yorker*. Then imagine some kid ordering the typical X-ray specs from an ad in the back of a comic book. The precedent exists for the omniscient device. The eyeglasses actually do allow the kid to see through clothing. The ring of familiarity will allow your reader to buy it. Only instead of sexy nakedness, the kid sees scars, bruises, the hidden proof of tragedy and suffering. His favorite teacher has a swastika tattooed on his chest. His best friend, the toughest boy in school, has a vagina...

Use what the reader already knows to gradually move to the fantastic. The tragic. The profound.

AUTHORITY: SUBVERT READER EXPECTATIONS

The linguistic anthropologist Shirley Brice Heath has said that readers value surprise above all else in a story.

If you were my student I'd tell you to create a clear scene. Render the setting and physical actions without judgment or summary. Use simple Recording Angel as if you were a camera. Allow your reader to determine the meaning of the events. Let your reader anticipate the outcome, then—boom—spring the actual intention, the surprise.

In chapter 20 of *Fight Club*, for example, we assume Tyler is bullying Raymond K. Hessel. As the scene unfolds, the reader assumes it's a robbery and that Tyler is taunting and humiliating the man, and that Hessel is a victim. People love this scene because it turns out that Tyler is practicing a form of tough love. First, he finds out the dream career that Hessel has abandoned. Then Tyler reminds the man of his mortality. Lastly, Tyler threatens to return and kill the man if he fails to take action toward achieving his dreams.

That scene was among the first I ever read in public, and the crowd response was jubilant. It ranks among everyone's favorite scenes in the film.

So direct and misdirect your reader, but don't tell her the meaning of anything. Not until she gets it wrong in her head. In "Guts" the narrator describes the climactic scene (pun intended) in fine detail, describing how an impossible serpent is trying to drown him in the swimming pool. This misdirection allows the reader to realize the truth before the narrator does. The horror is mixed with laughter as the narrator remains in denial until it's too late.

Always, always, if you were my student, I'd tell you to allow the epiphany to occur in the reader's mind before it's stated on the page.

Once on tour to England I shipped two thousand bacon-scented air fresheners in my luggage. These were cardboard squares printed to look like strips of bacon, and saturated in a bacon-smelling oil. They dangled from a string, designed for hanging from your car's rearview mirror. The Customs agent opened my suitcase and saw these and didn't blink an eye. I hadn't a change of clothes because there was no room left. As the two thousand people arrived for a reading in London, I handed each an air freshener. They opened them, handled them. Soon the entire hall smelled of frying bacon.

That night I read the story "Hotpotting," describing how young hikers will soak in natural geothermal pools. The story plods along until the narrator steps outside one night and smells meat cooking. Historically, the danger is that drunken people will slip into spring-fed pools, realizing too late that the water is boiling hot. The actual case histories are heart wrenching, and I detail several, gradually establishing precedent. Once the narrator smells bacon, it's too late. By then the auditorium stank of cooking bacon. Before they knew what the smell in the story heralded, people had jokingly rubbed the cardboard over their hands and faces.

The truth didn't have to be dictated. Any subsequent description would only confirm the dread they already felt.

It was a wonderful night, that night in London.

So never dictate meaning to your reader. If need be, misdirect him. But always allow him to realize the truth before you state it outright. Trust your readers' intelligence and intuition, and they will return the favor.

AUTHORITY: SUBVERTING MY EXPECTATION

One workshop, after my work had been rejected by some magazine or ten magazines or yet another agent had written to say he only represented "likable" fiction, Tom Spanbauer walked over to his bookshelf and studied the titles. He took down one book, then tucked it back. Pulled another, put it back, as if looking for the exact perfect book. At last he pulled a book off the shelf and gave it to me. "Read it," he said. "Next week we can talk about it. It will help your work enormously."

Don't look for me to name the book, a novel. A famous publisher, famous for only the highest-quality literature, had brought it out. The most prestigious imprint of a very respected house. The back of the dust jacket was crowded with the statements of famous writers praising the author and the work.

The following week I read and reread it. An easy job because it hardly topped a hundred pages, but a tough read because the characters were hard-pressed and put-upon cornpone hound-dog types just scraping by in the burnt-over backwoods hills of wherever. They lived on a farm, eating the same grits for breakfast every morning. They did nothing exceptional, and nothing happened to them. Each time I finished it I felt angry about wasting more time for so little return. I hated the author for wasting my time. But mostly I hated myself for being too backward to appreciate this work of art documenting the lives of folks interchangeable with the folks I'd been raised next door to.

The next Thursday I took the book back to Tom.

He asked, "Did you love it?" He didn't take the book from my hand, not right away.

"The writing was beautiful," I said. I hedged. What I meant was that the spelling seemed to be spot-on. Somebody had proofed the dickens out of this book.

He pressed, "But what did you learn from it?" Still not accepting the book.

"I don't think I understood it." I'd hated it. That, and I felt stupid for being too stupid to appreciate a book published by the smartest people in New York City. Clearly I'd failed. I felt like an oafish, uneducated yokel for not loving a book about oafish hillbilly yokels. It never dawned on me that maybe people in New York loved the book for the same reason that skinny white people love the film *Precious*. Because it makes them feel superior.

Other students were arriving and taking seats around

Tom's kitchen table. But he wasn't done. "What part didn't you understand?"

To fit in with the smart people, I lied. "You know," I said, "I really loved the language." If all else fails among the literati, always claim the language is beautiful.

Tom reached out and took the book. Workshop commenced. Who read that night, who knows? After the last comments about the last piece. After Tom read a few pages of what he was currently working on. Some students left. The rest of us opened bottles of wine.

It was Thursday night, my entire weekend rolled into an hour. We basked in the presence of this published author, living proof that a person could do this impossible thing. We drank, and Tom read. We argued about the Altman movie *Short Cuts* and whether it was true to Carver. Maybe we argued over *Magnolia* or *The Player*, both big movies at the time. At that I broke. "I hated it," I said.

Somebody, Monica Drake, maybe, asked, "You hated *Short Cuts*?"

No, I hated the book Tom had lent me. "So I'm stupid." It felt good to fall apart. The first step to being schooled toward some greater knowledge.

If you were my student I'd give you that same book and force you to read it and feel like an idiot for not loving it. Then I'd hound you about whether or not you'd loved it.

Because the next thing was, Tom smiled. "I didn't give you the book to enjoy."

He hadn't shelved it. The thing still lay on the table near his elbow. He looked at the cover and said, "This book is awful..." He grinned like he'd played a joke that never got old, no matter how many students he'd played it on. To me, he said, "I wanted you to see how terrible a book could be and still get published." He slipped the book back into its place among the books on the shelf, ready to be given to the next hopeless writer.

AUTHORITY: SUBMERGING THE I

If you were my student I'd tell you to read the story collection *Campfires of the Dead* by Peter Christopher. It was Peter who taught me about submerging the "I."

The theory goes that stories told in the first person carry the greatest authority because someone assumes responsibility for them. The storytelling source is present, not just some omniscient writerly voice. The trouble is that readers recoil from the pronoun "I" because it constantly reminds them that they, themselves, are not experiencing the plot events.

We hate that, when we're stuck listening to someone whose stories are all about himself.

The fix is to use first person, Peter taught me, but to submerge the I. Always keep your camera pointed elsewhere, describing other characters. Strictly limit a narrator's reference to self. This is why "apostolic" fiction works so well. In books like *The Great Gatsby* the narrator acts mostly to describe another, more interesting, character. Nick is an apostle of Gatsby, just as the narrator of *Fight Club* is an apostle of Tyler Durden. Each narrator acts as a foil—think of Dr. Watson gushing about Sherlock Holmes—because a heroic character telling his own story would be boring and off-putting as hell.

In addition, don't screen the world through your narrator's senses. Instead of writing, "I heard the bells ring," write just, "The bells rang," or, "The bells began to ring." Avoid, "I saw Ellen," in favor of, "Ellen stepped from the crowd. She squared her shoulders and began to walk, each step bringing her closer."

So were I your teacher, I'd tell you to write in the first person, but to weed out almost all of your pesky "I"s.

AUTHORITY: A CHARACTER'S BODY OF KNOWLEDGE

If you went out drinking with me I'd tell you how I used to measure money. When I'd first started writing, *Writer's Digest* reported that *Playgirl* magazine paid three thousand dollars for short fiction. That magazine seemed like the best market for a story I'd written called "Negative Reinforcement." At the same time a new building had been completed in downtown Portland, Oregon, the KOIN Tower, the new home of KOIN television and the many floors of luxury condominiums that rose above the broadcast studios. They were the swankiest address in town and each cost three hundred thousand dollars, so I did the math.

If *Playgirl* bought my story and ninety-nine more, I could afford a ritzy condo.

My point is that people measure stuff—money, strength, time, weight—in very personal ways. A city isn't so many miles from another city, it's so many *songs on the radio*. Two hundred pounds isn't two hundred pounds, it's that *dumbbell at the gym that no one touched and that seemed like a sword-in-the-stone joke until the day a stranger took it off the rack and started doing single-arm rows with it.*

As Katherine Dunn put it, "No two people ever walk into the same room."

We've already touched on this. While discussing ways to write from within a character's point of view, we considered that a painter walks into a very different room than a plumber enters. Some years back I was interviewed over the telephone by a Scottish journalist. Our conversation strayed to the music we'd liked as children, and he mentioned a Hall and Oates song that had always haunted him. The song described a girlfriend who was stealing food from her hungry boyfriend as he gradually starved to death.

A Hall and Oates song? It didn't ring a bell so I asked him to sing a line.

Over the phone he sang, "Every time you go away, you take a piece of meat with you…"

Another example from real life. A friend's daughter had her first menstruation, a trauma because to the girl it represented an end to her carefree childhood, not to mention the physical pain and the bother. My friend, the girl's mother, said that when the process was resolved, her daughter heaved a sigh of resignation and relief and said, "I'm glad that's only once a year!"

NO TWO PEOPLE EVER WALK INTO THE SAME ROOM

Katherine Dunn

Such moments are funny and heartbreaking. There's a joy in correcting some mistakes, but a tragedy in negating such a creative interpretation, especially one held since childhood.

My point is that our past distorts and colors how we perceive the world. If I hadn't said something, this man would've heard "meat" instead of "me" for the rest of his life. And how your character describes the world doesn't have to be based on anything factual. Actually, it's more interesting if a character views the world through a mistake.

Was it Kierkegaard? Was it Heidegger? Some egghead pointed out how people decide the nature of their world at a very young age. And they craft a way of behaving that will lead to success. You're praised for being a strong little kid so you invest in your strength. Or you become the smart girl. Or the funny boy. Or the pretty girl. And this works until you're about thirty years old.

After your schooling is over, you recognize your chosen way of winning has become a trap. And a trap with diminishing rewards. You're a clown no one will take seriously. Or you're a beauty queen who sees her looks fading. You're forced to realize your identity was a choice, and then to choose another. But you know this next strategy will never have the same passion as the one you'd chosen as a child. Now you're especially aware that it's a choice. And you know it, too, will likely fade. So many successful books are about a character leveraging youth and beauty for a good marriage, then leveraging that union for education, and leveraging that for wealth. A book like *Vanity Fair* or *Gone with the Wind* or *The Great Gatsby* depicts a social climber who navigates upward in the world by trading each asset for a greater asset.

The other choice the funny boy or the pretty girl can make is to deny the choice. To continue living according to the pattern for success he or she has established. But now that the trap is recognized, the funny boy becomes the bitter, snarky guy. He's the clever, hard-drinking put-down artist who lives to inflict pain. The pretty girl becomes the evil queen in *Snow White*, ready to destroy anyone who might be prettier.

Most of my own books are about characters who've reached the limits of one, early form of power. They've been the good, obedient boy (*Fight Club*) or the stunningly attractive girl (*Invisible Monsters*) and they've reached the point where they must find a new form of power. Or to continue, in bad faith, to live according to the old, failing pattern.

Think of Jay Gatsby, rejected by Daisy but already plotting to chase after her, to launch a fresh campaign to win her hand. Even once he knows in his heart that she's not such a great prize, he's too threatened by the idea of choosing a new dream.

Holly Golightly can't give up her strategy of always evading commitment, so she's doomed to roaming the world without emotional attachment.

Sally Bowles wants the love of the whole world so she rejects her suitor and is consumed by the chaos of Nazi Germany.

For perhaps the best example of this bad-faith choice, read Dorothy Parker's story "The Standard of Living."

So choosing a character's body of knowledge isn't merely

about how their past and their priorities color their view of everything. It's also about the pattern for success that they've chosen as children. The funny boy walks into a room looking for details to poke fun at, and listening for good setup lines he can riff off for laughs. The pretty girl walks in looking for potential competitors with clearer skin, better figures, brighter teeth.

If you were my student I'd tell you that *Playgirl* ultimately rejected "Negative Reinforcement." And instead of a luxury high-rise condo all I could afford was a three-hundred-square-foot shack in a neighborhood without clear television or radio reception. Cable television wasn't available, and the internet was decades away. The roof leaked, but in that tiny house with no distractions I wrote my first four books—five if you count the disastrous attempt *If You Lived Here, You'd Be Home Already.*

I'd ask you: What strategy has your character chosen for success in life? What education or experiences does he or she bring? What priorities? Will they be able to adopt a new dream and a new strategy?

Every detail they notice in the world will depend on your answers to the above questions.

A Postcard from the Tour

Did you see my Super Bowl commercial?

No, I'm not joking. It was a television commercial for a bank, slotted to air during the 2016 game, not nationwide, not like, say, a Budweiser beer commercial. An advertising agency pitched me on behalf of a bank, explaining that it would produce the commercial for a "regional" audience, meaning only a few million eyeballs instead of a billion, but the concept was simple. An actor would stand in the center of a bare stage and deliver a monologue lifted from my book *Fight Club*. The "We're a generation raised by television to believe that someday we'll be millionaires and movie stars and rock gods..." Yes, *that speech*, which Brad Pitt gives in the film. Short and sweet, followed by the bank's slogan, in voice-over, "Own your life or someone else will."

On the page, it sounded good. Okay, what sounded good was the money—they were talking six figures, a sum ten times what I made annually in my last day job. And the million eyeballs, those eyeballs would feel great. The only downside was the idea of selling out. My books aren't like cherished children to me, but I stand behind certain ideas. My counter-proposal was that, in lieu of an actor, I should be the one to deliver the speech. On television. During the Super Bowl. I should sell out in person.

Not to boast, but I'd been rejecting suitors for years. First was Volvo, poor Volvo, who asked me to write a series of enticing stories. This was in the age of "viral" internet advertising, and the stories would all center on an obscure hamlet in Sweden where an enormous number of Volvos were being sold. The concept could go anywhere, they assured me, but my impression was that an element of vampires would be welcomed. Each fragment of the story would be planted online, and the advertiser hoped the audience would coalesce around assembling the bits and discovering the ultimate reveal. They were offering, as I recall, tens of thousands of dollars.

I said, "No." In truth, you never say no. You say some polite version of "Thank you for thinking of me. This sounds like a terrifically exciting project; however, I'm overcommitted. Please keep me in mind for any future work..." Because you never know. This year's advertising designer is next year's movie director.

After Volvo came BMW with the proposal that I should write a collection of short stories. These would be recorded as an audiobook and provided on compact disc as a perk with the purchase of any new BMW. Once again, the money was enticing. Money always is. But I told them, "This sounds like a terrifically exciting project..."

Mind you, I'd read the castigating piece David Foster Wallace had written in response to Frank Conroy writing the copy for a glossy cruise ship brochure. Conroy had gotten his large family a fancy ocean cruise as payment, but later regretted writing the love letter used to sell similar vacations to his readers. But...but I'd also cracked my share of old *National Geographic* magazines and found full-page advertisements wherein Ernest Hemingway endorsed some brand of Scotch, William Faulkner flogged a certain cigar, and Tennessee Williams raved about—what else?—an ocean cruise.

Check for yourself. The ads are there. The greatest writers of the twentieth century weren't above hawking products. Why should I be?

It's not like I live in a cave. When Anthony Bourdain's people emailed my people and suggested I escort Tony— insiders called him Tony—on a tour of Portland, Oregon, sights, I agreed. Trouble is, to be on location with Tony was to find yourself a small float-y bubble in the surging sea of energy that rushed and broke around Mr. Bourdain. As we walked past restaurants, the wait staff would rush out and grab him, dragging him bodily in, settling him into a seat and delivering every item on the menu.

If you watch the reruns you might notice me hovering in the edge of some frame. If you look closer you can tell I've taken two 600-milligram Vicodins, and I'm high as a kite to deal with the stress. I stumble and mumble, and when we visit Voodoo Doughnut and they present me with a huge penis-shaped doughnut that spurts goopy custard all over my face, well, I'm unfazed.

In my defense, the next time Tony's people called and asked if I'd do an encore on his new show I sidestepped. Vicodin was in short supply so I suggested they contact the thriller writer Chelsea Cain, a friend of mine who knows Portland much better. Chelsea is smart and funny and telegenic, and they Googled her, and they opted not to book her for the show. Their reason? Chelsea didn't deliver a male demographic, aged eighteen to thirty-five. Something like that. As it turns out I do deliver those eyeballs. It wasn't me they wanted, not *me*, it was my readers.

And it's not as if I hadn't made a huge effort to whore myself already. One lunch in Chicago, my publisher set me beside Terry Gross with the specific instructions to captivate her and earn myself a slot on her popular National Public Radio show. All through that lunch I feigned interest in her cats, yes, cats, while psychically begging her to love me and interview me. Now, my guess is that show will never happen. Big sigh.

And it's not like I didn't accept some money along the way. In the year 2000 or 2001, Chevrolet offered me five thousand dollars for the right to mention *Fight Club* in a television commercial for the Ram pickup truck. Small potatoes since once my agent's commission was subtracted, as well as taxes, the payday amounted to less than I'd forked over for my first used car in 1978. A Chevy Bobcat (look it up). It seemed karmic, like Chevy paying me back.

Then Jaguar/Land Rover came calling. They offered me a half million dollars to write a story that could be made into a film that would feature a Land Rover in some crucial, high-profile way. A half million dollars. I thought of throwing myself at Terry Gross over lunch. I'd done worse things for money. And maybe I was stupid, but I still said no.

Not a year after that, the Super Bowl came calling.

It was flattering. Had Cheever ever gotten a Super Bowl spot? For that matter, had Shakespeare?

The advertising agency considered my idea for all of two minutes. It would mean paying me a licensing fee for the book excerpt. And it would mean paying me an additional fee to perform. And without batting an eye, they withdrew the proposal.

That's why you did not see me midway through the 2016 Super Bowl. It's not that I was too dignified or my principles were too high. It's that I asked for too much money, I don't deliver enough eyeballs.

But I still sit here. I'm not young, not anymore, but my phone is turned on. Just in case Volvo or Jaguar or Terry Gross calls. I'm begging: Please tell me, again, about your cats.

AUTHORITY: USING PHYSICAL SENSATION TO CREATE REALITY

Consider that your body has a memory of its own. And your body can tell stories. We love forensic science programs, where an expert walks into a crime scene and "reads" the clues. Under the scrutiny of Sherlock Holmes or Miss

Marple, details that seemed innocuous take on importance. In the same way, a doctor can read a mole or a twitch and diagnose something ominous.

Most stories engage the reader's mind or heart, his intellect or emotions, but few also pull in the reader's entire body. Stories that do elicit a physical reaction—horror, pornography— are seen as low culture. But if you were my student I'd ask, Why can't a high-culture story engage the mind, the heart, *and* the body?

Years back, a reporter for *USA Today* was interviewing me at The Ivy in Los Angeles. We sat on the patio screened by latticework and bougainvillea, drinking iced tea. She was friends with Tom Hayden, the political radical and second husband of Jane Fonda, and said Tom wanted me to come up after lunch and talk anarchy. He was fascinated by *Fight Club* and wanted to discuss it over a game of croquet. Yes, croquet. And the entire time the reporter pitched me on radical political lawn games she continually used the fingers of one hand to circle the slender wrist of her opposite hand. She'd pinch the wrist, making her fingers like a tight bracelet around it.

At a lull in the conversation, I called her attention to the mannerism. She looked down, surprised, as if her hands belonged to a stranger. She hadn't been aware of the behavior. As a teenager, she explained, she'd been anorexic. And as her body's percentage of fat decreased she'd determined little tests to measure it. At 2 percent body fat, she'd been able to feel the hollows between the ligaments in her wrist. This is what her hand had been doing: gauging her body fat. It had become such an automatic behavior that she still caught herself doing it. Or in this case, I had.

This is the kind of physical "tell" that, if you depict it effectively, you can prompt your reader to adopt. We are natural mimics. In high school I worked at a movie theater with another kid named Chuck. We weren't friends and seldom talked, but he had this nervous tic. The corner of his mouth would spasm slightly, pulling sideways. It was seldom still. Just that one corner jerking toward his ear.

Experts talk about "neural mirroring" or the tendency for a person to echo back the expressions and energy of another. Zombies, they say, are so frightening because they always display a flattened emotional affect. They show no emotion despite the circumstances. And the fact that they don't mirror the emotions of people makes them appear all the more hostile and alien.

Whatever the case, I hadn't worked with the other Chuck a week before I'd adopted his twitch. This wasn't deliberate. Not like when young people pick and choose from the mannerisms and traits they find appealing, assembling their own presentation. No, the mouth twitch was contagious.

That, that's the kind of physicality I'd tell you to develop in your work.

To heighten that physical element of a story, it helps to depict characters using drugs, or suffering illness. Depict sex and violence, or medical procedures.

These are all ways to exaggerate a character's physical awareness, and to prompt the reader to have a sympathetic physical reaction. Whether it's drugs or sex or illness, it also allows you to distort the normal world so that regular settings and events appear warped and menacing. The rose and the oak tree become the grotesque alien realities Jean-Paul Sartre saw them to be. In my story "Loser" a college student tripping on LSD participates in a television game show, and in struggling through he realizes that the competition to amass huge amounts of consumer goods is insane.

In E. B. White's story "Dusk in Fierce Pajamas" the onset of pink eye drives the narrator progressively mad with fever as he pores over the pictures in fashion magazines.

Tom Spanbauer would call this "going on the body." By this he meant focusing on physical sensation within a character. As in, "This would be a good place to go on the body..." It's a reliable way to unpack a dramatic moment. Just shift from describing the exterior scene to depicting the interior of a character. As the writer Matthew Stadler advises, "When you don't know what comes next, describe the interior of the narrator's mouth." He was joking, but he wasn't.

If done well, this prompts a similar reaction in the reader's body. With that complete, you can shift back to describing the scene, or intercut with a big-voice observation, or add a new stressor, or whatever you think will best keep up the tension of the moment.

By going "on the body" you enroll the reader's body as well as her heart and mind. You usurp his entire reality.

If you were my student I'd tell you to watch what people do unconsciously. Collect the stories they tell to explain their behavior.

For further examples, see the section that follows.

AUTHORITY: BREAKFAST AT
BROOKS BROTHERS

When my mother died I asked around until someone recommended a Jungian analyst. My aim was to tackle this mourning thing head-on.

Jungian because Carl Jung's storytelling approach appealed to me, dreams and all that, like keeping a dream log. And every Thursday morning before any of the downtown shops had opened I met this man in his high-rise office. He made me a cup of tea, and we talked about whatever frustrated me that week. I paid him three $50 bills and left vibrating with shame about talking too much and saying nothing significant while resenting how he'd said almost nothing.

His dog was old, he told me. He'd talk about saving its shed fur. A company on the internet would spin the dog fur into yarn and knit him a sweater he'd have to comfort him once the dog had died. A charming idea, still not worth the kind of money I was paying. This went on from around daffodil time until the first tulips bloomed, roughly from the Super Bowl until taxes were due.

Whatever an analyst does, he did it, if that includes watching the birds on the window ledge and occasionally asking if I'd had any dreams. I hadn't. The silence seemed like a waste of $150 so I kept filling it. An hour would go by, and I'd find myself waiting for the elevator, my throat aching from so much talk about nothing. The walk to my car took me past Brooks Brothers where one morning a sign in the window announced a sale.

Yeah, I had money to throw away on small talk and urban bird-watching, but Brooks Brothers? Some invisible force field kept me walking.

By then I'd talked out most of what I'd known about my parents, both dead. And maybe that was the strategy: to talk until the emotional attachment was exhausted. He'd sneak looks at the clock I knew stood on the bookshelf behind me. The sale signs still filled the window at Brooks Brothers. One morning I went in. At the clearance rack I found a brown tweed blazer and the salesman stood behind me and slipped it onto my shoulders. The sale price was $150. A tailor with a Russian accent waved me into the fitting area and said to step up on a low platform.

"Not like that," he said, "stand naturally."

Not like a military cadet, he meant. I stood with my shoulders back, my chest thrust forward, and my stomach sucked flat.

He meant: relax. His lips pursed tight to hold a row of straight pins, he chalked the cuffs and pinned the extra fabric between my shoulder blades. To borrow from Craig Clevenger, I felt as if I'd taken a Vicodin. My body felt warm. I relaxed into nothing less than a Holly Golightly trance. Whatever he was doing, this Russian tailor, pinching the shoulder padding. Patting the front to see if the buttons needed to be relocated. I couldn't remember the last time I'd felt this safe. It felt as if nothing bad could happen, not here with the polished wood paneling and houndstooth check, the madras golf shorts and Shetland sweaters.

An aside—in my childhood I marveled at how churches

were left unlocked all day. Some, all day and night. Our church, St. Patrick's, had no lock on the front door until I was a teenager. You could go inside and feel safe and collect your thoughts. Now only shops keep such hours so it's no surprise that shopping has become our comforting pastime. The twenty-four-hour supermarket has replaced the twenty-four-hour sanctuary.

The alterations would be done in a week, he said, and carefully slipped the jacket, bristling with pins, off my back. When I went to collect it, I bought a pair of slacks. They, too, needed to be pinned and chalked. The tailor was just walking in, apparently, undoing a chinstrap and taking off a black motorcycle helmet. I stood on the platform and he knelt to pinch and chalk. My analyst wanted to move our sessions to Wednesday morning, but I said I couldn't make Wednesdays. My therapy, such as it was, had ended. I wasn't cured, but I was free.

The next Thursday I bought another jacket, this one gray with a faint blue plaid. It was the one that fit the worst. Requiring three return trips for letting out and taking in. That early in the morning I was the only customer. The tailor would arrive in his helmet. Sometimes I'd see him shucking a black leather motorcycle jacket. He'd assess the new issue: the vent in back hung wrong, or the lapels wouldn't lie exactly flat against my chest. It was always something. And when it wasn't, and the jacket fit…then I bought another jacket that didn't fit.

My body knew something my mind didn't, and I wanted to understand its secret. Why did these straight pins, this greasy smell of tailor's chalk, and the sort-of yoga of standing stock-still, why did it flood me with this bona fide, genuine bliss?

Not then, but years later I'd be in Milan. My dentist had sold me on this ultrasonic toothbrush, saying it would be as good as the flossing I refused to do. Every thirty seconds the brush beeped to prompt me to move it to a new area of my mouth, and after two minutes it automatically shut off. Taking an electrical anything to Europe is a pain so I took my old toothbrush to Italy. There, the first morning I started to brush and brush, brush and brush. My mouth foamed red and I continued to brush. Rubbed raw, my gums bled. Still the toothbrush would not shut off. I took it from my mouth and looked at this, my old-school manual toothbrush, just a plastic stick with bristles at one end, and I told myself, "This thing must be broken!"

More recently I put my fingertip to a paper page of student work. I slid my finger down the margin thinking, *Why won't this scroll?*

Because it's paper! Because my electric toothbrush was back home! This is the autopilot manner in which we live our lives. Another time, a darker time, friends had rented a beach house, and we shared it for a weekend. Drinking, playing board games. During Trivial Pursuit, the wife half of a husband-and-wife team ventured a wrong answer and her spouse jumped to his feet, shouting, "Damn you! This is just like you, Cindi!"

The young couple flew at each other, cursing. Faces red, teeth bared. Recounting every past injury or mistake. The rest of the players froze and shrank into themselves, avoiding eye contact with each other as the storm raged across the table.

As the shouts subsided, I found I'd risen from my chair. I'd leaned into the fracas. Not to argue or participate, but to…bask. It felt as if this fight were a blazing yuletide hearth or a Thomas Kinkade "Painter of Light" comfort-porn landscape of some perfect thatched cottage in a twilight rose garden. My body responded, yearning, drawn forward by some dark nostalgia that the rest of me had forgotten.

The shouting, the curses. This fight wasn't one of my parents' many fights, but my body didn't know that.

That weekend I knew I had to explore my fear of and attraction to conflict. The vacation house hadn't enough beds so I'd been sleeping in the back of someone's car. And it was there, that weekend, I began to write *Fight Club*.

Do you see what I've done here?

If you were my student, I'd push you to create an epiphany. You'd have to dredge up or dream up the moment I realized why the tailor at Brooks Brothers had provided me with more comfort than a fortune spent on Jungian analysis. Me, I can't recall just one revelation so I've redirected you to other examples of physical memory. The toothbrush. The paper page that wouldn't scroll.

Did I tell you that my mother sewed our family's clothes? I'd forgotten that. But if my mind had forgotten it, my body had remembered.

Throughout my early childhood my mother had sewn clothes for my two sisters, my brother, and me. Every evening she'd call one of us upstairs from the basement television so she could measure and pin. First with the tissue-paper pattern pieces, then with the cut cloth. The standing still seemed to take forever, making each of us miss some *ABC Movie of the Week* (*Killdozer!* starring Clint Walker) or *McMillan & Wife*, *Columbo* starring Peter Falk, *Starsky & Hutch* starring David Soul, or *The Wonderful World of Disney*.

Her lips clamped tight around a bunch of pins, she'd stretch one corner of her pincushion mouth to say, "Hold still!"

My skin recognized the quick blunt slash of tailor's chalk. The peril of sharp pins. This Russian tailor with his motorcycle and black leather gear, he wasn't my mother, but my body didn't know the difference.

By then, by then clothes stuffed my closet. I had one cream-colored blazer, shot through with fine pink and blue lines, perfect for wearing with any of my dozens of Brooks Brothers pink or blue dress shirts. It looked great on the Tavis Smiley program. I had seersucker sport coats. A heather plaid I wore onstage at Carnegie Hall. Portland is not a place where men dress up so most of my coats and slacks went on tour, making their debut on television in Germany or Spain.

My pin-striped Brooks Brothers pajamas, so Dagwood Bumstead from the *Blondie* comic strip, I wore those for two years of touring with fellow writers Chelsea Cain, Monica Drake, and Lidia Yuknavitch doing our evening of "Adult Bedtime Stories." At the Ritz-Carlton in Houston and the Four Seasons in Baltimore, we'd drink in the hotel bar after each show, me in my snazzy pajamas and the women in gauzy negligees trimmed with hazy egret feathers. Our chests glittered with huge rhinestone brooches I'd found in Wichita, in an antiques store run by two ninety-year-old drag queens who were aging out of the drag queen business. Lidia and Monica and Chelsea wore retired drag queen necklaces that fanned as wide as peacock tails. At The Peninsula in Chicago, a diamond-studded and tuxedoed elderly couple, fresh from the opera, stood and glared. Loud, for our benefit and for the entire bar to savor, the man declared, "That is *not* appropriate attire for The Peninsula!"

If you were my student I'd tell you about the first writing exercise Tom Spanbauer typically assigned his writers. He'd tell them, "Write about something you can hardly remember." They'd start with a scent. A taste. One tangible physical detail would elicit another. It was as if their bodies were recording devices far more effective than their minds.

To repeat: Your body is a recording device more effective than your mind.

After I recognized the magic of the fitting room, it seemed less powerful. The tailor went back to being a guy with a cloth tape measure looped over his shoulders. From here my brain took over. The reason I'd always avoided buying clothes, even after I could afford to shop at places like Brooks Brothers and Barneys, was because it felt like an insult to wear anything nicer than what our mother could sew. Late nights, she'd baste and hem, calling a kid upstairs to test the size of a waistband. But despite her efforts—one night she fainted from heatstroke and our father found her sprawled between the ironing board and the Singer sewing machine— our clothes looked homemade. The fabric had been on sale because it was garish. The buttons had been recycled from a wedding gown or whatever. But to wear anything nicer we risked hurting her feelings.

So my clothes, even after my success, came from thrift stores.

So did my language. Store-bought clothes and ten-dollar words felt pretentious and show-offy so we bought what we could find secondhand, my siblings and I, and we talked about the weather.

And realizing that autopilot tendency set me free. My mother was dead. I could dress up a little. My ideas could grow because my vocabulary could.

So if you were my student, I'd tell you to listen to your body as you write. Take note how your hand knows how much coffee is left by the weight of the cup. Tell your stories not simply through your readers' eyes and minds, but through their skin, their noses, their guts, the bottoms of their feet.

AUTHORITY: HEW TO YOUR ARCHETYPE

Chelsea Cain and I both have huge suitcases we only use for long book tours. When I'd retrieve mine from storage the sight of it would make my dogs begin to cry. Chelsea's dogs, as she opened the suitcase across a bed and began to pack it, her dogs would climb into it and fall asleep among her folded clothes.

This prompted a story idea. In so many families a parent is

compelled to make long work-related trips…so, what about a story where the family cat climbed into the suitcase? The departing traveler boarded an overnight flight to Europe, and when he landed he found a text or voicemail from his spouse saying the cat was missing. Dread mounts. He gets to his hotel and can't bring himself to open the suitcase. Most likely, the beloved cat is inside. He doesn't want to find out if it's alive or dead.

The story resonated with me because it demonstrates the philosophical paradox of Schrödinger's cat. Look it up.

The cat story could be the entire story—ending with the man weeping beside a locked suitcase. Or pressing his ear to the side. Or forlornly petting the side of the suitcase. Or, being merciful, he finds the dead cat and phones his wife to say the cat's *not there* therefore it must be in the home, still. Or…?

Or the cat isn't a cat. Their toddler loves her daddy so much that she climbs into the suitcase. The man is oblivious and disconnected while flying to Europe. In London he's met by the police who demand to look in his suitcase. Or he finds a frantic voicemail from his wife—their child is missing.

Whether it's a cat or a baby inside the suitcase, whether it's dead or alive, the story is still a depiction of the Schrödinger's cat paradox. That's the archetype. And that's why readers will readily engage with it.

The lesson is: if you can identify the archetype your story depicts, you can more effectively fulfill the unconscious expectations of the reader.

In the story "Phoenix," I create the circumstance where a

mother demands a father hurt their child to prove his love for her. She's away on a business trip and their daughter refuses to speak to her over the phone. Fearing the child is actually dead, she demands her husband hurt the girl because a cry of pain would prove the girl is still alive. Ludicrous and horrible as it sounds, the story works because it's a retelling of the story of Isaac and Abraham from the Book of Genesis in the Old Testament.

But instead of God demanding Abraham prove his love by stabbing Isaac with a knife, it's a distraught mom pressuring a dad to stick their kid with a needle.

It's similar to using cultural precedent to move the reader from the known to the unknown, but somehow deeper.

If you can identify the core legend that your story is telling, you can best fulfill the expectation of the legend's ending.

AUTHORITY: GET SOMETHING WRONG

Among the easiest ways to gain the reader's trust is to get something wrong.

To my way of thinking, there are two forms of authority. The first I call "head authority," where the writer demonstrates a wisdom or knowledge beyond the reader's. This can be something basic and earthy, like the passages in *The Grapes of Wrath* where characters use thin brass wire to compress piston rings while reassembling an engine. Or something less savory, like the mother in my book *Choke* who switches the largely identical bottles between boxes of hair dye, knowing the buyers will get hair some color they never expected. Head authority is based on knowledge, used for evil or otherwise.

The second type of authority is "heart authority," gained when a character tells an emotional truth or commits an act that shows great vulnerability. The character shows an emotional wisdom and bravery despite enormous pain. Often it involves killing an animal, such as the scene in my book *Rant* where a character must kill his pug dog when it manifests full rabies. Or the scene in Willy Vlautin's *Lean on Pete* where the narrator must kill an aged, crippled racehorse. In the Denis Johnson short story "Dirty Wedding," the narrator is waiting while his girlfriend undergoes an abortion. A nurse approaches to say the girlfriend, Michelle, is fine. The narrator asks, "Is she dead?"

Stunned, the nurse says, "No."

To which the narrator responds, "I kind of wish she was."

At that the reader is stunned, but "heart authority" is created. We know the writer isn't afraid to tell an awful truth. The writer might not be smarter than us. But the writer is braver and more honest. That's "heart authority."

This occurs in my story "Romance" as the girlfriend's behavior becomes more and more erratic, and the narrator is forced into such denial that he must reject his friends and family. "…and after all that there's a lot less people at our wedding than you might think."

Emotional authority also comes through doing something horrible but necessary for a noble reason. It's the main character, Rynn, in *The Little Girl Who Lives Down the Lane* who is forced to kill those who want to molest her. Or it's Dolores Claiborne in Stephen King's book of the same name, who tries to kill her suffering, suicidal employer.

A character's mistake or misdeeds allow the reader to feel smarter. The reader becomes the caretaker or parent of the character and wants the character to survive and succeed.

Another way to create heart authority is to depict a character talking about herself in the third person. Think of the scene in *Fight Club* where paramedics are arriving to rescue a suicidal Marla Singer. As she's fleeing the scene, she tells her would-be saviors not to bother and calls herself irredeemable infectious human waste. In the play *Suddenly, Last Summer* the character Catherine Holly says, "Suddenly, last winter I began to write my diary in the third person..." In either case, the shift to third person implies self-loathing or disassociation or both.

So if you were my student, I'd tell you to establish emotional authority by depicting an imperfect character making a mistake.

A Postcard from the Tour

The arms started because of the tattoos. The ones the readers got. During my first book tours people would ask me, and I'd autograph their arms or legs. A year later we'd meet again. Another book, another tour, and they'd show me my signature made permanent in their skin.

My solution? To order wholesale. Arms, legs, hands, feet. By the cardboard caseload from slave labor factories in China. By the shipping container, in time. Gross after gross, if you'll forgive the pun. These are realistic, fake severed arms with gelatinous red blood and a yellowed stump of shattered bone where you'd expect. Jaundiced skin. In my Toyota Tacoma pickup I'd haul them home from the post office, a longish drive out twisting, two-lane Highway 14 through the woods. The one time, my first trip, I didn't think to tie down the stacked boxes. Two miles shy of my driveway a box disappeared from the rearview mirror, then another was gone. Where I could pull over, I looked back to the busted-open cardboard. The highway littered with bloody limbs. Cars and trucks backed up to the horizon. Nobody honking, they're so stunned to see me dashing around, throwing gory arms and legs onto the road's shoulder.

One log truck driver, the last vehicle to slowly crawl past once I'd cleared a path, looked down from his cab window and said, "You lost your first box three miles ago."

Most I found. A few I no doubt threw too far, their pink fingers and toes still hiding among the ferns, waiting for a hiker to discover.

Not intentional, but nothing to joke about, not in those woods where the Green River Killer and the Forest Park Killer had stashed their victims.

The bulk of limbs I'd gotten home where I sat on the porch and autographed them in the sun with a fat Marks-A-Lot pen. Nothing you'd want to breathe, indoors, hour after hour, neither the smelly rubber arms nor the pen.

Then off to the UPS Store they'd go, addressed to every bookstore on my next tour. So onstage at the end of each event I could call the bookstore staff up for a round of applause. Always following the applause with the same closing line, "Since you've given us such a big hand, we'd like to return the favor…"

Then the shared gasp of hundreds of people as we'd dump out the packing cases of autographed arms and legs and throw them like so much red meat for jumping readers to catch.

My answer to people wanting my name on an arm or leg. No more tattoos. In Ann Arbor one man hiked up his pant leg to show me my signature carved into his leg with an

X-Acto knife, but he was nice enough, not the maniac you might expect.

Every tour a well-oiled machine. Every tour another shipping container from China. In each city, "Since you've given us such a big hand..."

Until Miami one year where the book event was held on a waterfront stage owned by the Shake-A-Leg Foundation. Not that I knew that. How could I know? Not until I was introduced to the foundation's founder, after I'd thrown hundreds of severed legs into the crowd, and the founder turned out to be a handsome man, Harry Horgan, who'd been paralyzed in a car accident. Shake-A-Leg being his way to help others in similar circumstances. What could I do except apologize?

No offense intended. None taken.

Disaster averted. I get a lot of practice apologizing.

That, the only mishap east of the Mississippi. The west side, another story. All my western tour stops were scheduled, by chance, just one day after another writer, a man named Aron Ralston. Despite my labels DO NOT OPEN BEFORE PALAHNIUK BOOK EVENT, most stores were curious and opened the boxes early. Such a stack of mysterious, smelly boxes. They found all the severed arms and thought, *This is the most distasteful book promotion we've ever seen.*

And still not reading my labels, the booksellers went to Aron when he arrived and told him, "You'll be happy to know your severed arms arrived safely." Aron Ralston, the author of *Between a Rock and a Hard Place*, the book made into the James Franco film *127 Hours*. Yes, *that Aron*

Ralston. The man who was compelled to cut off his own arm while hiking. Who then had to politely tell the bookstore staff that they should read the boxes, and that the arms were for Chuck Palahniuk appearing the next night.

No shit, because in so many stores people had made this same assumption. And then the bookstore people somehow assuming I'd known my events would follow Aron's and that I was a deranged joker who'd methodically plotted to harass this other author, just out of my sick sense of humor.

When really, I'd been doing this for a few years. Simply to try and humorously dissuade some people from getting a tattoo. I'm really not a tactless dick, but maybe I ought to start to think more things through.

Tension

In real life writers are lousy at dealing with tension. We avoid conflict. We're writers because we like to deal with things *from a distance*. But writing still gives us a way to dabble. We create the tension. We manage it, and we resolve it. As writers we get to be the bully. If someone gets cancer, we caused it. Our job is to challenge and confront the reader, but we can't do any of that if we're so tension-averse that we can't create suspense and conflict.

As Ira Levin saw it, "Great problems, not clever solutions, make great fiction."

This means being able to tolerate the incomplete thing. Whether it's the unfinished first draft or the events confronting the characters. In regard to the unfinished draft, Tom Spanbauer used to say, "The longer you can be with the unresolved thing, the more beautifully it will resolve itself."

In regard to tormenting your characters, this is tougher than it sounds for many writers. Writers who come from a

GREAT PROBLEMS, NOT CLEVER SOLUTIONS MAKE GREAT FICTION

Ira Levin

background of abuse or insecurity might never get the plot off the ground. I've seen a lot of characters drink soothing tea while petting a cat and gazing out a window at the rain. And I've seen just as many characters exchange tennis-match quips that never rise above being clever. It takes some practice to create, sustain, and increase chaos, and trust that you can also resolve it.

Consider how the traditional burlesque show alternates strippers with comedians. Sex builds tension. Laughter cuts it. So such a program will keep the audience happy by first arousing people, then exhausting them with the release of laughter. Likewise, girlie magazines are famous for their formula of mixing nude photos with raunchy cartoons. Once more, one element creates tension. The other lessens it.

If you were my student I'd tell you I understand your unease with tension. But writing fiction allows you to experience escalating conflict, controlled by you. Writing fiction will help you deal with tension and conflict in your real life.

TENSION: THE VERTICAL VERSUS THE HORIZONTAL IN A STORY

It was a television commercial for Skipper's Seafood that broke the logjam for me.

In workshop Tom Spanbauer would always lecture about the horizontal and the vertical of a story. The horizontal refers to the sequence of plot points: The Woodhouse couple moves into a new apartment, Rosemary meets a neighbor, the neighbor jumps from a window one night...etc. The vertical refers to the increase in emotional, physical, and psychological tension over the course of the story. As the plot progresses so should the tension ramp up. Minus the vertical, a story devolves to "and then, and then, and then."

One way that Minimalist writing creates the vertical effectively is by limiting the elements within a story. Introducing an element, say a new character or setting, requires descriptive language. Passive language. So by introducing limited elements, and doing so early, the Minimalist writer is free to aggressively move the plot forward. And the limited number of elements—characters, objects, settings—accrue meaning and importance as they're used repeatedly.

Tom used an analogy taught to him by his instructor, Gordon Lish. Tom called the themes of a story "the horses." He'd ask a student, "What are the horses of this?" In his analogy, if you were migrating from Wisconsin to California in a covered wagon, you'd arrive at Stockton with the same set of horses you'd started with in Madison. Another comparison was to a symphony: no matter how elaborate the score became, the original core melody would still be present.

Call me a slow learner, but I didn't get it. Not until one night after workshop when I went home and turned on the television. A commercial showed an exterior view of a Skipper's Seafood restaurant. It cut to a shot of smiling people eating fish with Skipper's branded soda cups placed prominently on their table. Smiling and skinny, they wiped their beautiful faces with Skipper's branded napkins. We cut to a smiling employee wearing a Skipper's branded hat and apron…more Skipper's packaging…steaming fried fish…just everything Skipper's, Skipper's, Skipper's.

The commercial never cut to anything like, for instance, a red rose or a horse running on the beach. Here was the same message repeated in as many different forms as they could imagine.

I got it. That was Minimalism. The horizontal of the commercial told the story of a family going somewhere to eat. The vertical brought you closer and closer to their happiness and the food, quickly engaging your emotions and appetite.

So if you were my student I'd tell you to limit your elements and make certain each represents one of the horses your story is about. Find a hundred ways to say the same thing.

For example, the theme in my book *Choke* is "things that are not what they appear to be." That includes the clocks that use birdcalls to tell the time, the coded public address announcements, the fake choking man, the historical theme park, the fake doctor "Paige."

I'd tell you to watch television commercials. See how they never show you a fat person eating at Domino's or Burger King? Watch how they ramp up the vertical in only thirty seconds.

TENSION: THE CLOCK VERSUS THE GUN

If your stories tend to amble along, lose momentum, and fizzle out, I'd ask you, "What's your clock?" And, "Where's your gun?"

On book tours in Germany, getting a big crowd in Berlin has always been a crapshoot. The rathaus might be empty five minutes before the event is supposed to start, then—blam—everyone arrives at the last moment. The same goes for Los Angeles. In Berlin the organizers always shrug and say, "Berlin runs by many clocks," meaning people have many options and they won't commit to one until the last moment.

In fiction the clock I'm talking about is anything that limits the story's length by forcing it to end at a designated time. In so many books a pregnancy is the clock. In *Rosemary's Baby* and *The Grapes of Wrath* and *Heartburn*, we know the clock will run approximately nine months. When the baby is born, it's time to wrap things up. It's natural and organic and the pregnant character adds tension because of her vulnerability and possible harm to the unborn. So much is at stake.

But a clock can come in many forms. If memory serves, in the movie *Bringing Up Baby* the clock is the assembly of a dinosaur skeleton. In my novel *Survivor*, told aboard a jetliner that will eventually run out of fuel and crash, time is marked by each of the four engines flaming out. They mark the end of the first act, the second act, the third act, and the end of the book. Friends of mine hated how the diminishing number of pages betrayed how soon a book would end. And because I couldn't change that aspect of a book, I chose to accentuate it. By running the page numbers in reverse I made them into another clock, increasing tension by exaggerating the sense of time passing.

Not all clocks act as countdowns. Some merely mark change. Take Scarlett O'Hara's waist, for example. As the book begins it's seventeen inches, the smallest waist in six counties. But as time passes, her waist size grows, becoming the method for measuring time.

And a clock can run over the full course of a book, or just a single scene. Remember my novel *Snuff* and the sex doll slowly leaking air? That's a clock. A kind of air-filled hourglass. The moment the doll becomes a flat, pink ghost…time's up.

In the film *Se7en* the clock is seven days. In the film *Session 9* the clock is five days. Each time span is set to heighten tension by assuring the audience the story will not drag on.

As an aside, Billy Idol gave an interview wherein he commented on why so much punk music sounded the same. The typical punk song started at full throttle, ran for two and one-half minutes, and stopped abruptly. Only when I heard that did I realize how much the punk aesthetic had influenced my writing. This was the reason my best stories began with a jolt, seldom ran over ten pages, and ended by falling off a cliff. In so many ways I'd internalized the punk clock. A form as rigid as haiku.

In every story about the *Titanic*, the voyage is the clock. To make this clear to everyone in the audience, some stories place a thumbnail, like a summary or primer, on the front of the story. In the film *Titanic*, for instance, the oceanographers show a computer model of the ship sinking. They give a blow-by-blow description of what's about to happen. That distills the horizontal of the plot so the audience won't be distracted trying to analyze those inevitable events. Likewise in the film *Citizen Kane*, we see the entire plot summarized in a newsreel that plays in the beginning. We're told what to expect and how long it will all take. This way the viewer is less distracted by what happens. The analytical mind can relax, and people can engage emotionally.

In the movie *The Ring*, we're told, "You're going to die in seven days." And the mysterious videotape gives us the thumbnail summary of the entire discovery process. As the main character moves through the seven days we're thrilled to recognize each of the visual landmarks we were primed to look out for. All these same summary tricks work in the Sam Raimi films *The Evil Dead* and *Drag Me to Hell*. Now meta horror films like *Scream* and *Cabin in the Woods* use clocks based on the tropes of earlier horror films.

You'll see this type of thumbnail introduction used less in fiction, perhaps because it's so vague and trivializes events. Used well, it can be a good tease, hooking the reader with the promise of things to come. A great example is Spanbauer's *The Man Who Fell in Love with the Moon*, which opens with a boy doing morning chores while the upcoming plot is summarized in brief references. Another example comes from my book *Rant*, in the opening where a character summarizes the entire plot in a ridiculous explanation for how to qualify for a reduced-rate "bereavement fare" airline ticket.

A good clock limits time, thus heightening tension. And it tells us what to expect, thus freeing our minds to indulge in the emotion of the story.

A gun is a different matter. While a clock is set to run for a specified time period, a gun can be pulled out at any moment to bring the story to a climax. It's called a gun because of

Chekhov's directive that if a character puts a gun in a drawer in act 1 he or she must pull it out in the final act.

A classic example is the faulty furnace in *The Shining*. We're told early on that it will explode. The story might stagger on until springtime, but for the fact that…the furnace explodes.

In *Fight Club* and *Choke* the gun is the lie told to gain the sympathy of a peer group. The disease support groups or the would-be Heimlich maneuver-ers. When I wanted the story to collapse, I merely had to reveal the main character as a liar, and allow his community to redeem or destroy him.

Whereas a clock is something obvious and constantly brought to mind, a gun is something you introduce and hide, early, and hope your audience will forget. When you finally reveal it, you want the gun to feel both surprising and inevitable. Like death, or the orgasm at the end of sex.

Another perfect American gun…In *Breakfast at Tiffany's* the gun is Sally Tomato, the gangster in prison whom we meet early and soon forget about. Pages and pages go by without a mention of him. Finally the story is forced to chaos when the female lead is arrested and charged with aiding this organized crime kingpin. To a lesser extent, the story includes the two requisite deaths. First, Golightly's brother, Fred, who's killed in a Jeep accident. Second, the miscarriage of her unborn child as a result of the runaway horse incident in Central Park.

Also consider that the Second Act Sacrifice is a form of gun. It's the inevitable death of a lesser character that signals the move from comedy to drama. It's the death of Big Bob in *Fight Club*. It's the abortion in *Cabaret* or the best friend, Hutch, in *Rosemary's Baby*.

In *They Shoot Horses, Don't They?* the clock is the ever-dwindling number of contestants in the dance marathon. The gun is Red Buttons's heart attack—it triggers Susannah York's mental breakdown and the story quickly devolves to chaos. Just for the record, Buttons is the classic good boy character, career military, still wearing his navy uniform, and his death is more or less self-induced. Suicide, in a way. While Jane Fonda is the rebel who must be executed. As in *One Flew Over the Cuckoo's Nest*, the witness is also the executioner, and he tells the story in unusual flash-forwards that make little sense until the story's end.

But hold up. Don't let me get ahead of myself, here. We'll revisit the concept of the good boy, the rebel, and the witness.

For now if you came to me and said your novel was approaching eight hundred pages with no sign of ending, I'd ask, "What's your clock?" I'd ask, "Did you plant a gun?"

I'd tell you to kill your Red Buttons or Big Bob and to bring your fictional world to a messy, noisy, chaotic climax.

TENSION: USE UNCONVENTIONAL CONJUNCTIONS

Consider how an excited child tells a story. The sentences just cascade, one after another with few clear breaks. Such momentum! Almost like music, very much like music, like a song.

You can mimic this enthusiasm by using unconventional conjunctions to link together run-on sentences. Yes, you could use "and" repeatedly; I do so in my story "Romance." But there are infinite pseudo-conjunctions waiting to be invented.

In my story "The Facts of Life" I chose to use the two-word phrases "even if," "even when," "even so," and "even then" to mimic the sound of a drum machine in 1980s New Wave music. Specifically the Psychedelic Furs' song "Heartbreak Beat." As the endless sentences tumble forward, there's the constant regular beat of "even *something*" to keep time.

Similarly, in the story "Dad All Over" I insert the word "Dad" just to interrupt sentences. I force the word to become a form of onomatopoeia like "bang!" or "pow." The word becomes the drumbeat within the song, increasing in frequency to simulate how songs increase pace, also suggesting—I hope—the way a child will call out again and again for an absent parent.

Every story is an experiment.

In the story "Let's See What Happens" I create run-on sentences with increasing momentum by using the words "now," "next," and "always" to link verb-driven clauses. The effect is exhausting so I'm careful to alternate these relentless run-on passages with more conventionally written scenes.

In the story "Loser" I wanted to rely on sentences that seemed to contradict themselves midway. For example, "The box looks red, only it's blue." Or, "Sally reaches for a stick, except it's a dead snake." By repeatedly using the words "but," "only," and "except" I can create a sense of rhythm and the absurd, constantly stating and contradicting my statements in the same sentence.

So if you were my student, I'd urge you to cut your narrative like a film editor cuts film. To do this, you can use a repeating chorus: "The first rule of fight club is you don't talk about…" Or, "Sorry, Mom. Sorry, God." Thus cuing the reader with a sort-of touchstone that indicates: We're about to jump to something different.

Or you can keep the action flowing and increase the momentum of the energy by using a regular series of unlikely conjunctions.

If you were my student I'd tell you to listen to a child. Listen to someone who's terrified of being interrupted and has developed tricks for hogging a listener's attention nonstop. Granted, their stories might be boring, but you can learn some natural tricks for rolling your own fiction on and on and on.

TENSION: RECYCLE YOUR OBJECTS

If you were my student, I'd tell you to recycle your objects. This means introducing and concealing the same object throughout the story. Each time it reappears, the object carries a new, stronger meaning. Each reappearance marks an evolution in the characters.

Perhaps the best definition is by example:

Think of the diamond ring in Nora Ephron's novel *Heartburn*. We first see it while the narrator's riding the subway in

New York, en route to her group therapy session. A stranger winks at her. She worries he's a mugger so she twists the ring around so it looks like a plain gold band. She slips it off her finger and drops it into her bra. At the therapy session she finds the mugger has followed her. Brandishing a gun, he robs everyone in the group, finally pointing the gun at her chest and demanding the ring. The police take a report, and the ring is forgotten.

The ring reappears in flashback. When she gave birth to their first child, her husband gave it to her. During the labor, their newborn almost died, and now they're a family with the ring symbolizing the greatest moment of their love. Here the ring is described fullest, as a huge snowflake, something of incredible brilliance and value.

Much later in the novel, after endless events, after we've forgotten the ring, the police call to say they've caught the thief and recovered it. The narrator claims it and finds a stone is loose — an omen, she remarks. She takes it to the jeweler who first sold it to her husband, and he marvels over its beauty. Offhand, he says he'd always buy it back at a good price. Impulsively, she sells it for fifteen thousand dollars. That's the amount of money she needs to walk out on her failed marriage. Again, the ring appears, disappears, appears, disappears, appears, and disappears, each time to serve a new purpose in the plot.

That's what I call recycling an object in a story. The reader is thrilled to recognize something that seemed lost. And because the object is not a character and can't have an emotional reaction, the reader is forced to express any related emotion.

Another fine example is the ring in *Breakfast at Tiffany's*.

It appears as something worthless, a child's toy buried in a box of Cracker Jack. The protagonist's former husband gives it to her future suitor, and the ring disappears. Once the suitor is dating Miss Holly Golightly, the ring reappears as an object they can have engraved at Tiffany's. It disappears into the jeweler's hand, and only reappears at the moment of greatest crisis. Then the suitor produces it—now engraved—and presents it. It fits. In the film, they fall in love. In the novel, Golightly accepts the ring but is lost.

Also consider the gold cigarette case in *Cabaret*. It's offered by the rich man to the poor man, is rejected and disappears. It reappears, falling out of the rich man's pants, and is hesitantly accepted. Note: Anytime an object falls out of a man's pants, guess what that implies? Of course, the poor man is seduced by the rich man. The last time we see the cigarette case the poor man is compliantly lighting the rich one's cigarette. Note: In parallel action, the rich man has given a fur coat to a woman, and the coat is sold to pay for an abortion. It's a shame that the cigarette lighter remains unresolved in a similar important use.

Now consider the dog, Sorrow, in *The Hotel New Hampshire*. It dies. It's stuffed by a taxidermist. It falls from an exploding jetliner. Washes up on a beach. Is found and dried with a hair dryer. Wrecks a sexual tryst. Hidden away, it's eventually found and prompts a heart attack.

The dog's name alone prompts a major chorus in the book: "Sorrow floats."

Lastly, consider the green velvet draperies in *Gone with the Wind*. Miss Ellen's portieres are a symbol of status and of the matriarch herself. After the family has fallen on hard times and Miss Ellen is dead, her daughter pulls down the drapes and sacrifices them to make a gown she hopes will prevent the family from losing their greatest source of power, their land. One symbol evolves to become another.

An aside: In a forensic unpacking of the era, green was a popular color, deep green, because rooms decorated in emerald green seldom harbored houseflies or fleas, spiders or any other pests. For some miraculous reason you could leave windows open and green drapes seemed to repel mosquitoes. Families such as the O'Haras could lounge in their deep-green sanctuaries, unbothered by yellow-fever-carrying insects. Unknown at the time, emerald green or "Paris Green" dyes contained heavy amounts of arsenic. The deeper the color, the more poisonous the fabric. Up to half the velvet's weight could be arsenic, thus six pounds of Scarlett O'Hara's dress might contain three pounds of dissolved arsenic.

Green draperies, wallpapers, upholstery, and carpets killed any bug that came near them. Those people who dwelled in those rooms developed the wan, pale appearance the Victorians prized as a status indicator. Now picture Scarlett sashaying off to seduce Rhett, her dress steeped in poison, her face becoming more pale by the minute. After she's rejected, she charms Frank Kennedy and gets caught in an Atlanta rain shower. Soaking wet and coated in arsenic, Scarlett's least worry should've been paying the taxes on Tara. She's not unscrupulous, she's a walking victim of sick building syndrome. Such causal connections occur as little payoffs, providing your reader with joy and relief.

This takes morphing an object—the curtains, the dress, the shroud of mind-warping poison—in a postmodern or metafictional direction, but if you can get away with it, do so.

In my own lesser way, the liposuction fat in *Fight Club* becomes soap to be sold for money to finance the movement. Then it becomes nitroglycerin to be used by the characters to topple buildings.

So, my student, today's lesson is to recycle your objects. Introduce them, then hide them. Rediscover them, then hide them. Each time you bring them back, make them carry greater importance and emotion. Recycle them. In the end, resolve them beautifully.

TENSION: AVOIDING TENNIS-MATCH DIALOGUE

If you were my student I'd tell you to be clever on someone else's dime. You're not Noel Coward. Cleverness is a brand of hiding. It will never make your reader cry. It seldom makes readers genuinely belly laugh and never breaks anyone's heart.

So avoid tennis-match dialogue. That's where one character says something, and another responds with the perfect quip. Think of situation comedy dialogue. Snappy comebacks. Perfect rejoinders. Setup and spike. Instant gratification.

Tension is created and instantly resolved. So it never accumulates. The energy remains flat. For example: Wendy snuck a glance at him. "Do you have herpes?"

Brandon looked away. Gradually, his gaze came back to hers. "Yes. I do."

Question answered. Conflict settled. Energy returns to a big, boring zero.

Instead, if you were my student I'd tell you to never resolve an issue until you introduce a bigger one.

For example: Wendy snuck a glance at him. "Do you have herpes?"

Brandon looked away. Gradually, his gaze came back to meet hers. "I bought those place cards you wanted."

Or, "Wendy, honey, you know I'd never hurt you."

Or, "Geez! If you could just hear yourself!"

Or, "That Megan Whitney is a liar."

To which Wendy replies, "Who's Megan Whitney?"

To which Brandon responds, "I bought those place cards you wanted."

Always keep in mind our tendency to avoid conflict (we're writers) and to cheat and use dialogue to further plot (a cardinal sin). So to do the first and avoid the second, use evasive dialogue or miscommunications to always increase the tension. Avoid volleys of dialogue that resolve tension too quickly.

Again, it's not just me telling you this. Sitting on the floor in a quiet corner of an auditorium at Portland State University, Ursula Le Guin once gave me some advice. We were both speaking at an event for the Ooligan small press program. I'd told a story about taking a woman—an interviewer from

Italian *Vogue*—to an amusement park. First I'd brought the reporter a huge bunch of Mylar balloons. Once inside the park she let them loose and they drifted away. An explosion boomed. The park's rides slowly ground to a halt, leaving screaming kids trapped high in the air. It was chaos as sparks rained down and firefighters brought ladders to rescue the stranded.

The Mylar balloons had wrapped themselves around the main transmission line that delivered power to the area. High above us, the Mylar sputtered and melted, dripping flaming gunk. The park employees were cursing because they were out of work for the day, and all the concession food was spoiling. No one knew we'd brought the balloons. The reporter and I had slunk out, undiscovered. That was it. The story just fizzled on that vague note.

After I left the stage Ursula sought me out. We'd never met, but she wanted to help me brainstorm a better ending. Doing so she told me, "Never resolve a threat until you raise a larger one."

TENSION: DO NOT USE DIALOGUE TO FURTHER THE PLOT

Think of those low-budget television movies where the lieutenant rushes into the war room and says, "The Martians have breached our force field and begun destroying New York with a heat ray!"

Feel cheated? I know I do. Even if the lieutenant's uniform

Ursula K. Le Guin

is scorched from a deadly heat ray and his face is a charred mask of exposed bone, and he screams his announcement and falls dead...I first want to see some scale models of Manhattan being bashed and torched.

If a plot point is worth including, it's worth depicting in a scene. Don't deliver it in dialogue. You're not Shakespeare limited to the stage at the Globe Theatre and the endurance of the groundlings' legs. You have the budget and the time.

Even in an otherwise good movie like *Chinatown*, where the discovery process is patiently and meticulously allowed to demonstrate how water is being stolen for Los Angeles, the biggest plot reveal is done through dialogue. Evelyn Mulwray's daughter is a child of incest. Yes, it would be tons creepier if we used a discovery process to unpack *that* reveal—first speculating about the child's father, then tracking down a birth certificate, hearing rumors from former servants, exploring why Evelyn has no mother—ask yourself, which would be more dramatic? The history of water distribution in Southern California? Or the emotionally engaging discovery of father/daughter sex and the threat of grandfather/granddaughter molestation?

It sounds harsh, but I forbid you from furthering your plot with dialogue. To do so is cheap and lazy.

Years ago Tom began a workshop session by describing a public reading he'd done days before. He'd been asked to read with a very young writer, practically a teenager, who was in the process of writing a novel called *After Nirvana*. The novel depicted adolescent hustlers soliciting sex in order to buy drugs. Tom talked in awe about how the writer, Lee

Williams, unpacked a sex scene in a pornographic bookstore. Tom said he was amazed, wondering, *Is he really going to go there? Is this guy actually going to describe a kid giving an old man a blow job?*

And Williams did. He didn't redirect to something safer, for example having the narrator distract himself with the comforting childhood memory of eating a nice hot dog on July 4. Nor did he jump ahead to a future scene and recount the sex using dialogue or tasteful snippets of memory. Nope, the writer unpacked the details and read them in public to a crowd. Tom admired him for having the courage to write the tough stuff. And to read it. And if you were my student I'd tell you that that is your job.

To quote Joy Williams, "You don't write to make friends."

It doesn't make me look like anyone's bright, shining god when I stand up and read the "Guts" story. In many ways it's an act of public suicide. But good writing is not about making the writer look good.

So unpack the big stuff. Do not deliver important information via dialogue.

TENSION: NO THESIS STATEMENTS

Imagine a stripper walking out onstage, shucking his or her pants, and saying, "This is my junk. Any questions?"

Whether it was Channing Tatum or Jenna Jameson, you'd feel cheated. As readers or exotic dance enthusiasts, we want tension. We want a gradual discovery process. The outcome

Joy Williams

is more or less predictable: genitals. So we want sustained arousal and engagement.

It's a common mistake to give away everything in the opening sentence:

Lilla arrived at the barn dance a few minutes late, but just in time to see Reynolds kissing on Dawn Taylor.

Sure, there's a smidgen of tension. Who does what next? But everything is so summarized the reader hasn't had the pleasure of discovering anything. The payoff is in the first sentence. We don't know what the barn looks like, or smells like. We've no idea how Lilla feels, if her shoes hurt, or if she's been waiting tables all day. We're just—blam—dropped into the action.

This summary might work in comedy, where constantly negating drama creates humor. But even the best jokes rely on creating tension and then resolving it very quickly. Sometimes it's a long buildup full of power reversals, for instance:

A businessman arrives at his hotel and checks into his room. He opens the minibar and pours himself a Scotch, then dials the number of an escort service. When a voice says, "Hello," he interrupts. Fast, before he can lose his nerve, he demands, "Listen. I need you to send over the biggest, blackest stud you have and the skinniest, whitest nerd you have. I want to watch the black guy fuck the white guy, and then to watch the white guy fuck the black guy. And then I want to fuck them both. You got that? Can you make that happen?" At the pause, a polite voice, a familiar voice says, "Sir, you've reached Reception. You'll need to dial nine for an outside line…"

A long setup. The plot broken down into simple actions. The man in power asks for a display of power. Then he asks for a reversal of that power. Then he plans to overpower everyone. Finally, he's humiliated and left without power. So even humor needs to create tension for its strongest effect.

Consider that each sentence should raise a small question. As the smaller questions are resolved, they should raise ever-larger questions. A dancer removes her white gloves. He removes his necktie. She begins to unzip the back of her dress. He shucks his dinner jacket.

An opening creates a question and promises it will be answered, but not too quickly. Consider the first line of *Gone with the Wind*. "Scarlett O'Hara was not beautiful, but men seldom realized that when caught in her charm…"

It instantly makes you wonder, *Why?* You're hooked.

TENSION: NO DREAMS

As Tom explained this, Gordon Lish forbid depicting dreams in fiction. His thinking, as I understood it, was that dream sequences are a cheat. Reality can be just as surreal. Look at anything by Nathanael West.

Arbitrary as it might sound, nobody wants to hear about your dream from last night. Not even Carl Jung, unless you're paying him $150 an hour, and even then he's faking his interest. Dreams are fake, and fake stuff creates no tension. Fiction is already fake stuff so you don't need to water it down with faker stuff.

Remember, you came to me. You asked my advice on writing, and I'm telling you what I was taught: no dreams.

TENSION: AVOIDING FORMS OF IS AND HAVE AND THOUGHT VERBS

According to another article clipped from *Scientific American* and sent to me by a reader, a study demonstrated that people respond differently to different types of verbs.

When they read an active, physical verb like "step" or "kick" or "grabbed," the verb activates the part of their brain responsible for that movement. Your brain responds as if you're actually swimming a stroke or sneezing.

But when you read any form of the verb "is" or "has," no corresponding brain activity occurs. Likewise with abstract verbs such as "believe" or "love" or "remember." No sympathetic cognitive mirroring, or whatever, takes place.

Thus a passage like, "Arlene was at the door. She had long, brown hair, her face had a look of shocked surprise. She was taller than he remembered..." is less engaging than, "Arlene stepped into view, framed by the open doorway. With one gloved hand she brushed her long, brown hair away from her face. Her penciled eyebrows arched in surprise..."

With that in mind, I'd tell you to avoid "is" and "has" in

any form. And avoid abstract verbs in favor of creating the circumstances that allow your reader to do the remembering, the believing, and the loving. You may not dictate emotion. Your job is to create the situation that generates the desired emotion in your reader.

TENSION: THE SECOND-ACT ROAD TRIP

Once you've exhausted your standard settings, consider gathering your characters and sending them into the great outside world for some fresh perspective.

The road trip at the end of the second act works. Look at *The Great Gatsby*. Almost all of the main characters arbitrarily jump in cars and drive into Manhattan where the emotional showdown occurs in an overheated suite at the Plaza Hotel. Myrtle isn't present, but she sees their cars passing. And this tense, drunken scene nicely bookends the earliest dinner party at Tom and Daisy's house, where Myrtle interjects herself by telephoning. As the group returns from their Plaza foray, Myrtle throws herself in front of Gatsby's car, triggering the chaos of the third act.

In *One Flew Over the Cuckoo's Nest* the inmates of the asylum go deep-sea fishing accompanied by two prostitutes. When they return, Billy Bibbit has sex with one and kills himself, triggering the chaos of the third act.

In my own book *Fight Club* the narrator goes into the world to hunt for Tyler Durden, only to discover that he himself is Durden. This truth triggers the suicide/murder.

So once you've established your characters and settings, give your people a glimpse of the outside world. It's based on Heidegger, sort of, and his idea that escaping from your Dasein or destiny is pointless. The larger world reminds characters of their smallness and mortality, and it prompts them to take disastrous action. Think of the final flashback reveal in *Suddenly, Last Summer*. Sebastian finally takes action, but he's already doomed.

Perhaps this is why people dream of traveling a lot at retirement. Seeing the world and recognizing one's own insignificance makes it okay to come home and to die.

TENSION: RELIEF AS HUMOR OR JOY

If you were my student I'd tell you a joke. I'd ask, "What do you call a black man who flies a plane?"

As the answer, I'd shout, "*A pilot, you fucking racist!*"

What we think of as humor comes from the rapid relief of tension. First you think I'm going to say something hateful. And then I don't. In fact I reverse the accusation and throw it back at you. A classic power reversal.

A laugh or merely a happy ending occurs when you negate tension. The more tension you can create, and the longer you can sustain it without alienating your reader, the more satisfying the ending will seem. And even if you do alienate the reader, there's a good chance he'll return to the book out of unresolved curiosity. In 1996 when *Fight Club* was first launched, many book reviewers reported that they'd stopped reading at some point and had thrown the book against a wall—literally—but soon sought it out to see how it would resolve.

TENSION: EXPLORE THE UN-DECIDABLE

There is enormous tension in unresolved social issues. The French philosopher Jacques Derrida proposed that Western culture is binary. Things must be one way or the other. True or false. Alive or dead. Male or female. Anything that doesn't fall clearly into one category or another drives us to distraction. His favorite example was the zombie, which seems to be both dead and alive. As does the vampire. And in stories about either, the goal is to resolve them as dead.

This is the reason I depict questionable behavior in my work but refuse to endorse or condemn it. Why preclude the wonderful energy of public debate?

Often readers respond strongly without grasping why. Film historians speculate that Universal Pictures' *Frankenstein* and *The Phantom of the Opera* became hits because they allowed viewers an approved way to react to the lingering horror of World War I. Advances in medicine saved the lives of many soldiers who never would've come home from earlier wars. And these severely mutilated survivors occasionally appeared in public. These horror films gave audiences a scare, but they also allowed them to acclimate to the sight of "monsters."

Likewise, Bram Stoker's *Dracula* is said to have given readers an approved way to exhaust their fears about wealthy Jews who were emigrating to London in the nineteenth century. *Rosemary's Baby* safely pointed out how little control women had over their reproductive health at the time of its release. By couching his story as "horror," Ira Levin made it less threatening, less real.

With that in mind, consider other aspects of the culture that aren't clearly resolved. To me, what first comes to mind is abortion and male circumcision. People will fight forever to defend or denounce them. As a writer your job isn't to resolve an issue, but you can depict the situation and make use of the natural tension a topic carries.

As a writing prompt, consider a story about a man who wants his wife to have an abortion. She agrees, but only if he agrees to be circumcised. She'll give up a child if he'll give up a certain amount of himself, and quite likely some of his sexual pleasure. He won't have to raise another child. She won't have to bother with the floppy, droopy flap of male skin that's never quite as fresh smelling as she might like.

As another writing prompt, consider the canned meat Spam. The writer Doug Coupland tells me that anthropologists have a theory as to why the canned meat is so popular among Pacific Islanders. They speculate that Spam has a taste and consistency close to that of human flesh, and cultures with a distant history of cannibalism crave the product without realizing why. So…a secret dining club hosts ocean cruises where guests are taken miles offshore, into international waters, and pay a huge fee for a banquet of human flesh. The truth is the hosts actually prepare and serve Spam. Is it ethical to charge people—icky people, granted— an exorbitant fee for fake human flesh?

A final writing prompt: You're a college professor in physics or chemistry, and your most promising student comes to you with a discovery. She's found a new molecular property in chocolate. She's brilliant and naive, but you realize that her discovery could eventually be used to arm the most destructive bomb humankind has ever known. If she's allowed to publish her findings, sooner or later billions will die as a result. You caution her, but there's no guarantee she won't someday share her discovery. Should you kill her? And because you know, also, and might someday suffer dementia and let slip the deadly secret, should you kill yourself as well?

You get my point? If you were my student, I'd urge you to find some unresolvable issue that will instantly guarantee tension and debate over your work.

TENSION: STORIES THAT SPIN INTO MADNESS

This next type of story is among my favorites. They're short. They have to be short to prevent exhausting the reader. They offer the chaos and illogic of Kafka, but with the humor of satire. I won't spoil the surprise, but will save you a lifetime of hunting, for they are rare birds, indeed.

"Dusk in Fierce Pajamas" by E. B. White. A bedridden man, delirious with fever, becomes obsessed with the lives and images of the effortlessly rich celebrities he reads about in the pages of fashion magazines.

"My Life with R. H. Macy" by Shirley Jackson. A young

woman, possibly Jackson herself, becomes a lost, nameless cog as she trains for a job in the faceless bureaucracy of the world's largest department store. The antidote to her horror story "The Lottery."

"And Lead Us Not into Penn Station" by Amy Hempel. A litany of everyday absurdities and insults suffered in New York City.

"Reference #388475848-5" by Amy Hempel. The funniest attempt to get out of paying a parking ticket by anyone, ever.

"In Hot Pursuit" by Fran Lebowitz. A very chatty, snotty, gay Sherlock Holmes jets out to Los Angeles in search of an organized ring of pedophiles.

"Loser" by Chuck Palahniuk. A fraternity pledge takes LSD and is selected from the studio audience to play the game show *The Price Is Right*.

"Eleanor" by Chuck Palahniuk. A long string of malapropisms follow a logger as he escapes the deadly tall trees of Oregon only to meet his violent destiny in the stucco subdivisions of Southern California.

"The Facts of Life" by Chuck Palahniuk. A father attempts to teach the birds and the bees to his seven-year-old son, in a sex education lecture replete with self-immolating genitals and Sally Struthers.

If you were my student I'd assign you the following writing prompt.

Write as if you were the collective voice of a film review board that's been asked to assign an audience rating to a yet-to-be-released movie. Speaking in the collective "we" you cite increasingly absurd inferences the board members believe they are seeing. Clouds that look too phallic for comfort. The maybe-not-accidental way that shadows cast by people and animals combine and interact. Doughnuts being eaten by children in a possibly suggestive manner. In your report to the filmmaker, you cite how individual viewers first recognized each transgression, but when it was pointed out all reviewers seized upon each as a blatant offense. The story should be a snowballing litany of "projection" as the self-righteous viewers protest about subliminal horrors that demonstrate more about the reviewers' sick imaginations than anything actually depicted in the film.

Good luck. Keep it short. Go nuts.

TENSION: CREATE SUSPENSE WITH DENIAL

In old-fashioned literary terms, anytime you broach a subject yet refuse to explore it, that's called *occupatio* (in Greek *paralipsis*). For example, "The first rule of fight club is you don't talk about fight club."

But the technique also covers statements such as, "You know I'd never kill you, don't you?"

Or, "He told himself not to slap her."

Anytime you deny a possibility you create it at the same time. Such statements introduce the threat they appear to be denying. For instance:

This ship is unsinkable.

The canned salmon is supposed to be safe.

Please don't mention Daniel's murder. We're not going down that road.

As a writer, anytime you want to introduce a threat, assure the reader that it won't happen. Cross your heart and promise that that terrible, looming, unthinkable event will never take place. Instantly dismiss the possibility. That seems like a guarantee of safety, but it's a great way to introduce the promise of chaos and disaster.

A Postcard from the Tour

The first time it happened I didn't know it had happened. The room felt warm and crowded with people so no one was too surprised.

My goal was to match the power of Shirley Jackson's story "The Lottery." When it was first published in *The New Yorker* in 1948, hundreds of readers canceled their subscriptions. Nowadays the story is taught to children in school. That left me wondering: What would a story have to depict to generate the same level of anxiety today?

In Jackson's day I suspect that her story resonated with the military draft. The idea that we all live in peace and security due to the fact that randomly chosen young men are destroyed in the most torturous ways science can devise. Nobody ever says as much. When a book like *The Stepford Wives* hits big, people react to the surface details. No one dares mention how it keys off the ominous threat of a male backlash against the push for women's rights.

"The Lottery" is a classic, and people still ignore how its terror is the terror of millions of young men who hope for high draft numbers in some inevitable lottery. To name the thing, we'd be forced to deal with it.

Incidentally, I owned a portion of Jackson's cremated remains. Her daughter Sadie was friends with friends of mine through the San Francisco Cacophony Society. Sadie had been selling the cremains online, branded as "ShirleyBone," and she sent me a batch when she heard I was a fan of her mother's work. I opened the box at the kitchen table over the objections of my housemates who were eating breakfast. Ashes and crunched-up bone. Such a relic is too good to hoard so I found two antique boxes, carved wood inlaid with ivory, and divided Shirley between them. One I sent to my agent with a letter of provenance. The other to my editor.

All the while, I wondered what modern story could match the impact of "The Lottery."

Since college I'd carried the story of a good friend who'd tried "sounding"—look it up—with a rod of wax while masturbating. The bills for emergency surgery had ended his academic career. A decade later a drunken friend had told me about buying all the ingredients for a carrot cake, plus Vaseline. He'd ditched the sugar and flour, but had gone home to peg himself with the carrot—look it up—while he masturbated. Two good anecdotes with a common theme, but still not enough to craft a story from.

Finally, while researching my novel *Choke*, I met a man who'd almost died while pleasuring himself in a swimming pool. Here was the third element I needed. It took a Vicodin for me to write a draft in one marathon sitting. The first time I read it in our weekly writing workshop my friends laughed. It got a couple of groans, but nobody keeled over. In regard to a line about the dog, Greg Netzer said, "Thanks for the big laugh at the end."

The story, I called "Guts."

On the surface the story is shocking, but its power lies in how it depicts the alienation we feel as our budding sexuality alienates us from our parents. After it was published in *Playboy* magazine and in the *Guardian* newspaper—which lost numerous subscribers for showcasing the story in its Sunday supplement—a man wrote to tell me it was the saddest, most moving story he'd ever read. It's always heartening when someone looks below the surface.

Its first public reading took place at Powell's Books in the top-floor Pearl Room. That was a warm evening. I heard after the fact that a young man at the edge of the crowd had fainted. No one sets out to write a story that makes listeners faint.

The following night, at a reading in a Tigard, Oregon, Borders bookstore two people dropped where they were standing.

By Cody's Books on Telegraph Avenue in Berkeley I knew what to expect. The auditorium was packed. From the podium I could see the tension on people's faces, the irked look that comes from being too crowded together. Strangers were pinned shoulder-to-shoulder with strangers. Everyone resented one another for the overall discomfort. The heat and dankness and lack of personal space.

The local publicist, David Golia, had witnessed the faintings in San Francisco bookstores, and he swore they were triggered when I read the words "corn and peanuts." In Berkeley, when we arrived at corn and peanuts I noticed a young man sitting in the center of the audience. His head flopped to one side, and he slumped against the girl beside him. To judge from her expression they were strangers. Her face snarled in disgust at the physical contact. His torso toppled across her lap, and she cried out as he slid to the floor.

Her scream brought the focus to her. And I stopped reading as the rows and tiers of people all stood to get a better look. People clutched their hearts and cupped their hands over their faces. Clearly they were all concerned. As far as they knew he was dead. Those immediately around him lifted the man off the floor but there was no room for him except across the lap of the young woman who'd screamed.

From the podium the scene was a strange pietà. The seemingly dead man lay draped across the young woman's lap. Also present were elements of the Last Supper as the flanking people and everyone surrounding them, they all reached forward as if to help. Four hundred expressions of despair and empathy.

I looked at David Golia. We both knew what would happen next.

The fallen man blinked awake. Finding himself the center of attention, he blushed. People gently helped him to sit upright in his own seat.

And the crowd...they went nuts. Weeping. Applause. They'd forgotten I was even there. To them they'd just witnessed a death and resurrection. Lazarus. The tension vanished, and in its place was this warm sense of unity. They'd forgotten their resentment of each other and had become a community bonded by the experience. Already, they were telling the story to one another. Their shared horror and relief made them a family.

With the stricken man's permission I'd eventually finish reading.

In city after city, in England and Italy and wherever, it almost always followed that same pattern. Corn and peanuts. I quit counting the fallen when they reached a total of seventy-three, but I continued to read the story. Several times people fainted in line, silently reading it. People told me about fainting on subway platforms while reading. Recently, at the 6th and I Historic Synagogue in Washington, DC, five people passed out and were ministered to by a doctor in the audience. As I reached the end of the story the stained-glass windows were flashing with the red and blue lights of the ambulances that had arrived.

That's the story about the story. To date, hundreds have fainted.

I think Shirley Jackson would approve.

Process

People ask, "Where do you get your ideas?" Their question should be so much bigger.

Sometimes the premise occurs first. Other times, a single sentence or phrase is the genesis of an entire story or book. Once, a friend at my day job said, "I see the way you think things are." Such a wonderful-sounding sentence, full of echoes and ambiguity. I repeated the sentence at workshop that night and writers fought over who would use it first. On tour in Kansas City with Todd Doughty, beloved Todd, the greatest living publicist, he and I asked the ticket agent to check all of our bags under my name. I had a business-class seat so there would be no extra charge for Todd's bag. The ticket agent shrugged, cheerfully saying, "I've never done it that way. *Let's see what happens.*" Again, such a wonderful sentence, so filled with curiosity and anticipation. It became the title of a story in my coloring book *Bait*, illustrated by the fantastic artist Duncan Fegredo.

PROCESS: MY METHOD

In the 1850s the United States Coast and Geodetic Survey produced sketches of the California coastline for the purpose of siting lighthouses. Among the artists they hired to produce copperplate engravings was a young man who routinely doodled small portraits into the margins of his work. These were small studies, showing the effects of lighting people's faces from different angles. They're charming, but when they started to appear in official elevations meant to document the Santa Barbara coastline, they got him fired.

The man was James McNeill Whistler, and he went on to bigger things. But today those little figure studies show how a creative mind constantly works.

You never know when you'll encounter the remarkable idea, image, remark. The other day I was walking past a construction site where several bricklayers were working on scaffolding while a hod carrier hurried to supply them all with fresh mortar. It looked like a terrible job, running buckets of wet mortar up and down ladders. To show his appreciation, one mason shouted, "Dude, I love the way you keep the mud alive!"

Okay, that wasn't *just the other day*, it was eleven years ago. But that's how a wonderful sentence can stick in a writer's mind. It's poetry, the way the vowels and consonants repeat with such symmetry. Especially the v's that occur at each end. It's standard practice for writers to keep an "everyday book" in which to jot down ideas or useful trivia, but the best stuff sticks in your brain until you find a place to showcase it.

"Dude, I love the way you keep the mud alive." Now it's found a home.

At an event for National Public Radio in Portsmouth, New Hampshire, the funny, charming producer told me about dinner with the stoic family of a WASP friend. She silently mimed using a knife and fork to demonstrate how they ate the whole meal without speaking. In summation, she dubbed them, "New Englanders, God's frozen people."

How could I forget that? How could I not use it? Whenever I suffer through a silent, stultifying meal, I elbow a friend and say, "God's frozen people." Now that wonderful quip, too, has found a home.

For years I wrote back and forth with the writer Ira Levin. He endorsed my book *Diary*, and I was stunned to be in contact with the author of *Rosemary's Baby* and every other great book, plus the play *Deathtrap*. When I asked about his writing methods he wrote back, telling me a parable about a man with a very long beard. Once someone asked the man if he slept with his beard on top of or beneath the blankets, and he couldn't say. He'd never given it any thought. That night he tried sleeping with his beard under the covers but couldn't. Then he tried with his beard above the blankets, but couldn't. And after that the man never fell asleep ever again.

Ira Levin's point being: don't overthink your creative process.

But if you were my student, and you asked, here's what I'd tell you. First, I work best in boring places with little stimulation but with other people present. These places include airports. Car dealerships. Hospital emergency room waiting areas. While I still worked at Freightliner Trucks my earliest ideas were scribbled inside notebooks, sandwiched between the torque specifications, fastener sizes, and part numbers of whatever mechanical project I was assigned. Just as Whistler's sketches appeared on maps during his daytime job.

I think of myself as a conduit. I am the disposable thing trying to identify the eternal thing. Experience enters and product exits.

I acknowledge my mechanistic leaning. Years on the Freightliner truck assembly line color my process. Subassemblies are completed and feed into the main assembly line. These might be short stories that depict the major plot points. Each is an experiment to develop the book's voice. It's akin to collage.

An aside: Years ago I was taught that book tours were intended to drum up local media in large markets. Those were the bygone days of daily newspapers and local daytime television. Such media is all but gone. Today's writers will more likely be asked to produce a series of short essays that websites or magazines can use as content. In the United Kingdom that's long been the case. Instead of sleeping, a writer on tour in London will find herself spending the night in the hotel's business center, hammering out a dozen last-minute pieces about her favorite horror story, historical figure, and cure for writer's block. To avoid this pitfall, build your novel with a number of scenes or chapters that can stand alone as short stories. Magazines and websites can excerpt these, and they make a much better advertisement for your book. Plan for the fact that every medium wants free content.

Back to process…To begin a book or story, I collect the necessary parts by brain-mapping notes longhand in a notebook. I carry the book everywhere and jot any ideas or images or wordings that seem ideal for the scene or story. Once I have several pages I keyboard these notes into a file, cutting and pasting them to see how they work juxtaposed in different ways.

At this stage I print the full draft of the incomplete mess. I bind the pages and carry them everywhere, reading and editing them whenever I get a quiet moment. When next at my computer I key the changes into the file and print a new draft to bind and carry and continue editing.

A painter once told me that any artist must manage her life to create large blocks of time for creative work. By making ongoing notes throughout my day, when I finally do sit down to "write" I have a pile of ideas. I'm not wasting any of my valuable creative time by starting from zero.

I'll be continually bouncing ideas off friends and fellow writers in workshop. To see how readily people engage with the topic, and if people suggest new avenues or recognize patterns that hadn't occurred to me. And to make sure the idea hasn't already been used in popular culture recently.

When the story works somewhat, I look for holes where something extra is needed, like a beat of time or a smoother transition. An on-the-body moment or a telling gesture. Or where further research might help. Once the holes are filled, I've got a story that will eventually become a plot point in the future book.

In this way I create a few key scenes. Maybe depicting the character's job. How the romance begins, the "meet cute." Or the inauthentic way in which the character gets his emotional needs met, i.e., how he fools people into loving him. Each of these must stand alone as a short story. First so I can read them in workshop and test their effect, then garner feedback for revisions. Second so I can read them publicly and test where the energy lags or where hidden laughs occur. True story: When I read the story "Romance" on tour people always laughed at the line, "And we pitched my tent..." The characters were camping at a music festival, why was that funny? On tour someone explained that "pitching a tent" is the new euphemism for getting an erection. Go figure.

Self-contained, the story can also be sold to a magazine, for extra money and to assure some future book publisher that the topic has already been embraced by other editors.

These short stories accumulate. Each helps establish the verbal gimmicks of the narrator, and subsequent stories riff on those same devices. By now I'm printing all of the stories, binding them and carrying the collected work everywhere. By shuffling their order I can test the pacing, looking for places where an aside or flashback will help sustain tension or distract the reader before the surprise of a resolution.

This arduous process of creating a complete first draft, Tom calls it "shitting out the lump of coal." As in, "Relax, you're still shitting out your lump of coal."

Over time I'm carrying a full draft of the book. The most important plot points, the original stories, are done. The main structure of the fictional house is built and more or less watertight. What's left to do is to tweak the pace and try different endings.

The benefit to this method is that, initially, each story gives me a sense of satisfaction. I'm not carrying around the mess of an incomplete novel. As each story is finished and sold, I'm free to begin a fresh story. I know each subassembly works because it's being published or it's been applauded by an audience.

If I were your teacher I'd admit this sounds pretty artless. But if you hold a full-time job, have a family, and have to juggle every other duty in life, this scene-by-scene experimentation will keep you sane.

PROCESS: CROWD SEEDING

Another Freightliner story. In cold weather feral cats would come to live in the truck assembly plant, despite the constant roar of pneumatic tools and the mist of oil and paint that hung in the air. People would feed them from lunch boxes, and we'd glimpse them running between the shelter of one crate and the next. On occasion we'd open a carton to find a nest of newborn kittens, pink and mewing, and management policy required that any kittens be immediately dumped into the shredder. There they'd be instantly pulverized like so much cardboard or packing material. Policy or not, no one was that heartless. Even at the risk of our jobs we'd keep the kittens a secret, hiding them and feeding them until spring arrived and they could venture outside.

Every job is its own world. On my first day in that same plant my foreman sent me to another work station to retrieve some tool called a Squeegee Sharpener. The foreman at the next station sent me to another foreman who sent me to a fourth station in the line, but not before each foreman cursed me. By shift's end I'd been to every station in the plant, from rough cab buildup to offline, and met every foreman, and they'd all cursed me and spat on me. There was no such tool as a Squeegee Sharpener, but that's not the point. What's important is that I'd learned the layout of the place and had introduced myself to every boss I might ever be assigned to work for.

And the point of me telling you this story is that years later I told it at a party and everyone present almost leapt forward for the chance to tell almost the exact same story from his or her life. Someone who'd worked at Red Robin said on her first day she was sent around to find the Banana Peeler. Someone said that at Target he'd been sent to find the Shelf Stretchers.

You see, a good story might leave everyone in awed silence. But a great story evokes similar stories and unites people. It creates community by reminding us that our lives are more similar than they are different.

In fact a friendly competition begins. A man who'd worked in a brick factory in Toronto said he'd been told to fetch a bucket of hot steam. His co-workers had taught him how to cup a bucket over a steam tap, then run with the metal bucket upside down. He'd never questioned the task, but had spent his first day dashing around with blistered hands, trying to deliver steam where it was needed.

Another man said that television stations used to make

the new hire wash the lighting gels. These are thin sheets of colored plastic used to tint the lights on set. They're called gels because the originals were thin sheets of incredibly fragile gelatin. On your first day in television a station manager will give you a few sheets and tell you to wash them. If you scratch or tear them, you're told you'll be fired. You're sent into a janitor's closet with a sink and told to use the hottest water possible. Of course they give you the old type made of gelatin, and the moment the water touches them the sheets melt and vanish down the drain. The man telling me this, he'd spent the rest of his first day in television hiding from his boss, certain he'd be canned.

A pediatric surgeon said how during his residency he'd been paged one night. This was late, long after midnight, during a rotation that hadn't allowed for much sleep or food. He'd been napping on a gurney when the public address system had announced a Code Red and summoned him to a distant room on a seldom-used floor of the hospital. There, he'd stepped off the elevator hearing screams from the room in question, and as he entered he saw a naked woman in bed, covered with blood and holding a baby. The woman screams, "You! You killed him, you sonofabitch! You killed my baby!" She throws the dead infant, and he catches it without thinking. The blood is sticky and smells foul. The baby, heavy and limp. The room is oddly lit, with lights shining nightmarishly from under the bed and multiple partitions and drapes pulled halfway closed.

The reason for the drapes is because the entire surgical staff is hiding, watching. The woman in bed is a nurse. The dead baby feels so real because it's the doll used to teach artificial respiration. And the blood feels and smells real because it's real blood that's passed its expiration date. Everyone is crowded into this shadowy room because they want to see what was done to them...done to you.

These stories. Hazing stories. I'd tell the best ones, and strangers would try to beat them with true stories from their own lives. The culmination was in Paris. A man in a suit, wearing beautifully shined shoes, took me aside and gave me his business card. He was a veterinarian, and explained that becoming a vet in France was not an easy process. He'd applied to the academy seven times before being accepted. In celebration his advisers and instructors had thrown a party in his honor in one of the laboratories.

They'd drunk wine, and the group had congratulated him roundly on his entry into the program. And at some point someone had given him a glass of wine doctored with a sedative. Because this is the tradition. He'd fallen asleep, and they'd removed his clothes and trundled his naked, sleeping body into a fetal position. Then they'd carefully, meticulously tucked him and stitched him into the gutted belly of a newly dead horse.

"When you wake," he told me, "you have no idea where you are at." Your head pounds from the sedative. You're shivering with cold. It's dark and stinks so horribly you can't take a deep breath. You're compressed so tightly you can't move, and you want to vomit but there's not even space for that. Still, you can hear voices. Beyond this dark, cramped space your professors and advisers are still having their party, and the moment they see you move inside the tight skin of the horse they begin to shout.

"So, you think it's so easy to be one of us!" they shout. They taunt, "You can't just fill out some papers and become a veterinarian!" From all around you, unseen, they shout, "You've got to *fight to join our profession!*"

As they demand you fight, calling, "Fight! Fight!" you begin to struggle and push against whatever is binding you. And as you claw a hole in the tough, dead hide you feel someone press a glass of wine into your bloody hand.

Slowly, you're forced to birth yourself, naked and bloody, from this dead animal. And once you're out your companions cheer you and accept you with genuine warmth, and you continue, naked and bloody, to celebrate, having earned your place in their ranks.

This man in Paris, with his business card and shined shoes, explained why the tradition exists. This grotesque, age-old ritual. Because it creates a shared baseline experience that will someday be a comfort. In the future, no matter how many beautiful little puppies or kittens die under your care, no matter how heart wrenching your job might feel, it will never feel as horrible as waking up inside a cold, dead horse.

The best stories evoke stories. I call this "crowd seeding." Like the practice of cloud seeding, which produces rain, crowd seeding is a way to take a common, personal experience and test it, and develop it. None of us live such atypical lives that others can't relate.

Note: Cole Porter was famous not for inventing his catchy

lyrical hooks, but for overhearing them. He'd listen in public places, and he'd choose the most popular slang terms and build songs around them. People were already saying, "you're the top" and "anything goes," and that made it all the easier to sell his work. Similarly, John Steinbeck's method was to listen at the fringes. To study how people spoke and to learn the details of their lives. He panicked once he became famous. As the center of attention he could no longer gather what he needed.

Crowd seeding works in so many ways.

First, crowd seeding allows you to see whether a story engages people. Does it instantly hook them and resonate with their lives? Does it call to mind anecdotes they'd all but forgotten? And does it give them permission to relate stories they'd never dared?

That's important. Often people will withhold themselves out of fear of offending or being judged. But if you take the risk and make the first move, you give them permission to risk sharing. A small fish catches a bigger fish.

"Guts" continues to give people permission to tell similar true stories. One woman, a woman my age, told me how when she was in second grade she'd been a Brownie. This is a precursor to becoming a Girl Scout. She was seven years old, and got a stomachache, and her mother had put her to bed facedown on a vibrating, electric heating pad. "It must've slipped down between my legs," she told me, "because I woke up with *such a feeling!*"

She'd never experienced anything so glorious. She had no idea what had happened, but the next time she was to host the Brownie troop she'd said, "Brownies, you've got to try this heating pad!" They did, and after that every troop meeting was at her house.

"It was like *Sex and the City* for seven-year-old girls," she said. "For the first time I was the most popular girl in school." She beamed proudly. "And everyone wanted to be my best friend."

That's until the day her mother came home from work early and caught them all with the heating pad. Her mother sent the other girls home. "She yanked the cord of the pad from the socket in the wall," the woman told me, "and she beat me and beat me with it. The whole time demanding, 'What kind of a dirty whore did I raise?' and 'How dare you do such a filthy thing?'"

The woman confided, "I haven't had an orgasm since second grade... but if you can stand up and tell your story about jerking off with a carrot in your ass, then maybe I can go back to my mother and talk about the heating pad... maybe I can use that story instead of being *used by it*."

I wanted to correct her. "Hey, lady, the 'Guts' story didn't happen to me!" But who cares? Writing isn't about looking good. The point is to give people permission to tell their own stories and exhaust their emotional attachment and reaction.

Beyond testing a story's appeal and resonance, crowd seeding provides you with bigger and better examples that illustrate the same dynamic. Remember, Minimalism means saying the same thing a hundred different ways. My Squeegee Sharpener memory is cute, but it was the bait that attracted the steam bucket story, the gelatin story, the surgeon's story, and ultimately the French veterinarian's dead horse story.

Perhaps the best aspect of crowd seeding is that it allows a writer to work among people. So much of this job is done in isolation, whether alone with a pen or keyboard, or alone on a stage, or alone in a hotel room. It's always a joy to just introduce an idea and listen as other people perform. My degree is in journalism. I lack imagination, but I am a good listener, and my memory is decent. And for me writing fiction is about identifying patterns common to many, many lives.

So if you were my student, I'd tell you to go to parties. Share the awkward, unflattering parts of your life. Allow other people to share theirs, and look for a pattern to emerge.

PROCESS: MY KITCHEN-TABLE MASTER'S IN FINE ARTS

Tom always said that 99 percent of what any workshop does is give people permission to write. It legitimizes an activity that most of the world sees as pointless.

Every Thursday at Tom's ran the same course. We'd meet at his house at six in the evening. He'd ask each of us how we were, usually using the third person. Asking Monica Drake, "How is Monica feeling this week?" Asking me, "What's going on in Chuck's world?"

We'd socialize and Tom would share about his own week. He was a living, breathing author, and we craved his stories about book contracts and movie options. Just having Tom present made our own dreams seem possible.

The socializing allowed for stragglers to arrive. He'd give a lecture on some aspect of writing, like "horses" or "monkey mind versus elephant mind." Other times a guest writer would stop in and give a talk. This could be Peter Christopher teaching us to "submerge the I" or Karen Karbo telling us that a gun is never just a gun. It has to be particularized. She gave this lecture after hearing me read the first chapter of *Fight Club*, so I went back to *The Anarchist Cookbook* and found the details about making a homemade silencer, and my resulting gun worked infinitely better to establish my authority.

With all the students accounted for, Tom called for pages. It was the chorus we used for decades, "Who has pages tonight?"

A student had to bring printed copies for everyone to read as the writer read the work aloud. Part of this practice came from Lish's workshop at Columbia. It's agony to read your work and hear where it plods along. Part of reading aloud came from Tom's training with the Bowery Theatre in New York. There is no more honest feedback than laughter or groans or the motionless silence that genuine tension creates. That, and reading aloud prepares you for eventually reading in public on a book tour.

Listening writers would jot notes in the margins of their copies. After the reading, people had the opportunity to respond. Opinions were only useful if they came with a suggestion for a fix or if they praised a specific aspect. Cross talk was discouraged because we might spend all evening trying to dominate each other. As we became trained in Tom's distinctions—big voice, on the body, horses, sous-conversation, manumission—it became our language for evaluating a piece.

For the record "sous-conversation" (or subtext) refers to the message that's submerged in the actions and dialogue of the scene, the hidden extra meaning. Tom's use of "manumission" meant the grace with which your sentences carried the reader forward without disturbing the fictional dream. To demonstrate this, he'd cup his hands and tilt them as if gently passing a small object back and forth between his palms. A good writer must gently pass the reader from sentence to sentence, like a fragile egg, without jarring the reader out of the story.

The last to respond to student work would be Tom. He could always say something generous.

Always present was a good-natured sense of competition. If Monica made everyone laugh, I'd be determined to make them laugh harder in the week to come. Cross-pollination always occurs in a group setting. It wasn't unusual for one writer to introduce an endearing dog in a story, and within the weeks to come everyone's work would include an endearing dog. As much as Tom taught us, we also taught one another with our mistakes and successes.

We were young and hip enough to recognize when a writer's new idea was already cresting in popular culture. And we pooled our best insider advice about tax law and literary agents. For years we all trusted our tax returns to the same preparer, a woman who specialized in finding loopholes for emerging painters, musicians, writers, and other marginally profitable artist types.

The evening would repeat this pattern—students reading, everyone responding—until people were too tired to pay attention. Occasionally the phone would ring and wreck the mood of someone's story. I was adamant about Tom unplugging the phone, but he'd forget, and it would ring and sabotage the payoff of someone's perfect plot point. Usually mine. As students got better, no one wanted to read after them so the anchor person was usually Suzy Vitello, Monica Drake, Joanna Rose, or me.

Finally, Tom would read from his work in progress. No one was allowed to critique Tom's writing, no one dared. It was thrilling to hear something we knew would soon go into a real book. Or something we'd know, later, had been cut from the eventual final draft. Not unlike seeing the secret deleted scenes from a movie.

We'd applaud Tom, and he'd begin lighting candles. Candles on the table. Candles on shelves. Someone would pass out glasses and people would open bottles of wine they'd brought.

From that point it was a party. We'd talk about books, but mostly about movies because it was more likely several of us had seen the movie in question. We debated *Thelma and Louise*. *Boogie Nights*. *Prêt-à-Porter* ate up an evening. Tom lent us books or told us what to read. Story collections by Amy Hempel, Thom Jones, Mark Richard, or Barry Hannah.

As wine was poured Tom would rub his palms together in a loud, showy way and ask, "Okay, who owes me money?" We'd pay two hundred dollars in cash for ten sessions. When cash got tight, Tom took household objects in trade. He'd moved from New York and still needed furniture. I remember Monica in particular bringing a lamp...a vase...

The writer Steve Almond recently stated in the *New York Times Magazine* that writing workshops might be replacing psychoactive drugs as the new talk therapy for mental illness. By writing, people present their lives as fiction and tackle their issues as a craft exercise. By redeeming their protagonist, they find their own redemption.

Tom would agree. In his approach, called Dangerous Writing, he encouraged students to explore their deepest, secret, unresolved anxiety. The writing process would provide the reward of resolving those issues, making publication and sales—if they happened—a less important bonus. For me, the workshops served an even larger purpose.

Through our lives, our relationships are based on proximity. We attend the same school. We work at the same company or live in the same neighborhood. And when those circumstances change, our friendships dissolve. But at Tom's and in workshops since Tom's my friendships have been based on a shared passion. Instead of proximity, our mutual passion to write and share our work brings my friends together, largely the same group since 1990. Every week. That means seeing each other through marriages and new babies and someday grandchildren. Some among us have died. New friends have entered workshop. We've watched each other fail and succeed.

Back in the 1990s it was our party every Thursday night. And whereas my partying to date had been about binge drinking—toking bong hits and shotgunning beers to forget my boring life and job—this was a party that celebrated a new future. We were young, toasting our heroes. Our dreams would actually come true. We would all become authors.

PROCESS: THE GOOD WRITER AS BAD ARTIST

If you're going to be a good writer, don't be afraid to also be a bad artist. Ray Bradbury painted. Truman Capote made collages. Norman Mailer drew. Kurt Vonnegut drew. James Thurber drew. William Burroughs blasted paint-filled balloons with a shotgun.

Monica Drake, the author of *Clown Girl* and *The Stud Book*, paints the most perfect still lifes, in oil paints, on switch plate covers. She protects them with several layers of clear varnish, creating unlikely little masterpieces people come in contact with every day.

Consider that some form of visual art will complement your writing. To recover from the colorless, limited world of abstract language, spend some time working with colors and tactile shapes.

PROCESS: THE WRITER AS SHOWMAN

If I were your teacher I'd tell you to overserve your audience.

According to the linguistic anthropologist Shirley Brice Heath, the books that become classics are the books that bring people together in community. The Tolkien books, for instance, are famous for uniting like-minded readers who love them.

To create this community, give readers more than they can handle alone. Give them so much humor or pathos or idea or profundity that they're compelled to push the book on others if only to have peers with whom they can discuss it. Give them a book so strong, or a performance so big, that it becomes a story they tell. It's their story about experiencing the story.

Again, my core theory is that we digest our experience by turning it into stories. Repeating the story—good or bad—allows us to exhaust the unresolved emotion of it.

If you provide readers with something too strong to readily accept, they're more likely to share it. Community forms as people assemble to explore their own reactions. Charles Dickens knew this. As did Mark Twain. A book needs a face, and even the best writers have to act as showmen. Promoting a book is part of your profession so there's no point in hating the process.

Find some way to love every aspect of the writing job.

Somewhere around my bah-zillionth book tour I started to hate the tours. Between the sleepless nights in hotels, the early-morning flights, and the airport fast-food meals, I began resenting the people I was meeting. My solution? I believe that a physical gesture trumps a thought, so in Phoenix, Arizona, I asked the local publicist to stop by a Claire's shop, where I bought bags of rhinestone-studded crowns and tiaras.

The two most difficult parts of an author event are

prompting questions from the audience, and, finally, when too many questions are coming too fast, stemming the tide. My solution was to offer a tiara for each question. The barrage started instantly. Clearly I had only so many prizes so with the last crown, the questions ended. Best of all, I had a great time. I could not hate and resent people at the same time that I gave them lovely tiaras and whatnot. The act of giving something rewired my thoughts.

You see, the secret is to trick yourself into having a great time. Whether you're on a twenty-city book tour or washing dishes, find some way to love the task. In fact there's a Buddhist saying told to me by Nora Ephron, the one-and-only time I met her after reading her work since college. At a noisy Random House party in the restaurant Cognac, she said, "If you can't be happy while washing dishes, you can't be happy."

People wrote to me about how they wore their tiaras to school. So I expanded to the autographed severed limbs. Then the glowing beach balls. In Pittsburgh on the tour for *Damned*, the writer Stewart O'Nan gave me ten full-size candy bars that I threw into the auditorium that evening. It was such a good contrast to just talking. It felt great to throw things as hard as I could so I began to buy huge sacks of candy bars and to heave them at people. Few things mirror the delivery of a good joke or story better than watching the arc of a thrown bag of Snickers bars as it flies over the heads of a thousand people and lands in the arms of just one.

That did the trick. I loved doing events again. I'd spend all winter staging and shipping the props. The blow-up sex

dolls. The penguins and giant inflatable brains. To be honest, it cost me a fortune. Each big event set me back roughly ten thousand dollars in props, prizes, and shipping. But I'd ask, by a show of hands, how many people had never been to an author's book tour event. And always, it would be most of the auditorium, so it felt worth all the fuss to make these people's first book event something special.

I'm not sure if I'll ever stage such big events again, but I'll always be glad I did.

Also, if you were my student, I'd tell you to make the reader/author photos a story. For *Pygmy*, Todd Doughty, beloved Todd, the best publicist alive, he and I carted around a towering trophy. It broke down into many sections, and before each event I'd be in my hotel room screwing it together like a sniper assembling an assault rifle. All so that I could ask readers to hold it in photos. Forever after, when anyone saw the pictures that resulted they'd ask, "What did you win?"

Again, the photos would generate a story. The events would generate a story. If I did my main job well, the book would generate a story. And people will come together to tell their stories about the story. And that's the reason why I'd tell you to find a way to have fun at work, and to give your audience something they can't stop talking about.

PROCESS: LEARNING BY IMITATION

A common joke in Tom's workshop was that students followed his rules so well that eventually they all sounded like bad imitations of his best work. It's a joke, but it's true. And it must've been disheartening to hear this stream of unintended parody. His own narrative voice being used to tell stories to which he had no attachment, exaggerating his storytelling devices to the point of burlesque: it had to be soul crushing.

It was only natural. Most of us had started writing by trying to mimic Fitzgerald or Hemingway. I read and reread *The Portable Dorothy Parker* until her snark became second nature to me. Now we were aping Tom, and the best of us would ultimately merge elements of his style with the best of what we'd cribbed from other writers. We'd add a few tricks we discovered on our own, and we'd create a unique voice. Unique enough. A hybrid.

What's important is that imitation is a natural way to learn. In the golden years of Gordon Lish, when he taught at Columbia, edited for Knopf, and ran the literary magazine *The Quarterly*, he was known as Captain Fiction. His best students were the most promising young writers in America. And those writers wrote according to his demands and dedicated their work, publically, "To Q," meaning to Lish, and it was a juggernaut. Lish's unstoppable army.

Unstoppable until it was stopped. The critic Sven Birkerts, writing for *The New Republic*, called attention to how similar all the great, young Minimalists sounded. They wrote in the first person, in the constantly unspooling present moment, in "byte-sized" perceptions. And Birkerts was correct, and the shining edifice of Minimalism no longer looked like the future.

Just as Chick Lit fell out of fashion…Once a style or genre becomes too copied, reader fatigue kills it.

So no, the idea isn't to follow every rule of Gordon's and Tom's and mine, not forever. But it's better to start with some rules. Learn some compulsory skills. After that you can free-style, and if you're lucky and if you're successful a new generation of aspiring writers will copy your style and drive your hard-won, well-crafted voice right into the ground.

PROCESS: BUILD YOUR INFRASTRUCTURE

Even when you're written out, you can still do the work of a writer.

When you're between ideas, build the infrastructure you'll need. Among the best Christmas presents I've ever gotten is a robust three-hole paper punch that can handle twenty-five or thirty pages at a time. My career started in the days of paper manuscripts, and I still prefer to send my first complete draft to my agent and editor in hardcopy. That means stocking printer ink and binders. You'll eventually need mailing envelopes for contracts. A filing system for incomplete work.

No electronic storage system is foolproof. Chelsea Cain is the most tech-savvy writer I know, and she still lost a near-complete novel. It couldn't be found in the cloud or in any of the emails she'd sent herself as backup. Eventually she sent her hard drive to a company that specializes in recovering lost data for the military and even they couldn't save the lost book. My tech guy tells me that even flash drives often mysteriously scramble or lose information. So you'll want a way to print and file your work.

You'll want a system for organizing tax receipts. Like an engaged couple planning to get married, make a list of the tools and supplies you need. A sort of gift registry. And send it to friends and family. Better you should get a good-quality stapler and boxes of staples than some cologne you'll be rushing to re-gift. Let people know what you're doing, and allow them to help in this way.

Seriously, I cannot tell you how much I love my three-hole punch. And the four-drawer file cabinet I found used for five dollars. And the L-shaped 1960s "secretary's desk" enameled avocado green I bought for fifty bucks. It's so big that it filled half my apartment. A friend saw how it crowded my bed and remarked, "You have the only bedroom I've seen with a receptionist."

Yes, this is all very pedestrian. But get good task lighting. Develop a system for organizing your books and supplies. You won't dread handling paper correspondence if you have a stock of boxes, envelopes, a tape gun, and a designated table to work on. You won't dread tax time if you regularly total and bundle your receipts.

Being a writer consists of more than writing. The next great inspiration will come along, but until it does…clean up your desk. Recycle the old paper stuff. Make room for the new arrival in your head.

PROCESS: PUBLIC READINGS

Tom would arrange public readings. At coffeehouses, usually, one time at Common Grounds on Southeast Hawthorne Boulevard in Portland, a sold-out evening so well attended that the short-staffed barista gave Tom and me uniforms and we bused tables and washed dishes while the readings took place. Farther down Hawthorne Boulevard was Cafe Lena, which hosted an open-mike reading every Tuesday night.

Beware those long-established, come-one-come-all evenings, and be aware that the opposite of reading isn't listening. Instead, it's the drunken impatience and polite applause of a hundred poets each waiting his turn. There, people found their regular attention fix. Each week set a trap that caught the same writers. They never brought work to a larger market.

Of the readings Tom organized, one brutal night comes to mind. At a sports bar we took turns standing on the pool table to shout our stories against the noise of pinball machines and televised football games. The drinkers talked over us. One writer, Cory, sweet little Cory with her thick glasses, she shook while telling the story of her nephew dying of juvenile leukemia. Tears rolling down her freckled cheeks. The drunks shouted at the televisions, oblivious. These were video-poker-playing beer drinkers. No one gave a rat's ass about the well-crafted emotional striptease we were doing on their pool table.

My turn came, and I read a short story about waiters pissing in food before serving it to wealthy guests, what would someday become chapter 10 in *Fight Club*. By the end someone had turned down the volume of the televisions. No one played pinball. What's to say? A coarse story about piss and farts won them. They were listening, listening enough to laugh.

PROCESS: PIRACY

A few years ago, the assistant to Todd Doughty, beloved Todd, the greatest living publicist, decided to return to college for a graduate degree in writing for television. The young man enrolled at Columbia, and on his first day of classes sent Todd a photograph of the program's assigned textbook.

The title? *Chuck Palahniuk's Advice on Writing*. The book contained essays I'd written for Dennis Widmyer's site, The Cult. Years ago, the site's focus on me was unnerving, and I'd hoped to provide content that would redirect visitors to the craft of writing itself. In all, I wrote some thirty-plus essays, and the site kept them behind a firewall for subscribers to read. Nobody was making any real money. Whatever the case, they'd been liberated. The university had downloaded, printed, and bound them, giving them a title and a cover I'd never intended, and charging students for the use of them.

This isn't some Russian pirate site, this is Columbia University in NYC.

The discovery was flattering and frustrating and drove me to do what I always do in such no-win situations—I started crowd seeding. Introducing the topic into conversations with creative people who depend on the royalty income from their work.

In Mantova, Italy, I had dinner with Neil Gaiman, his daughter was just graduating from a college program there. He seemed resigned but hopeful on the topic: Gaiman proposed that if someone loves a writer's work, really loves it, that person will eventually buy it. He speculated that in the countries where such piracy was rampant the economies were terrible. As those economies improved and people had more disposable income, they'd someday begin to buy the actual books they enjoyed. Gaiman likened a free, pirated book to the first no-cost shot of heroin that, with luck, will create a lifelong addiction. He advised patience. The loss to piracy was just a cost of doing business.

This came to mind in Toronto, where a very tall man with a shaved head brought me a downloaded copy of *Choke* printed on standard-size typing paper and bound with Chicago screws. In a thick accent he said that my books and the books of Stephen King were the most popular novels in Russia, but that no one ever had to buy them. He then stood in line and refused to step aside until I autographed his "book."

To me it looked like a false economy.

Unless printer ink, paper, and binding are also free in Russia, it's likely this man had actually paid more to create his version than he would've paid for a commercially printed one. An irony he shrugged off. More recently a young couple from Ukraine told me the same. They described seeing subway cars filled with people who'd printed their own copies of *Fight Club*. When I mention this to my artist friends, they shake their heads.

As bad as writers have it with piracy, comic creators have their own special circle of hell.

Comic conventions are rife with hack artists who sell fans counterfeit prints of Hellboy or the Black Panther. These are versions drawn by amateurs, drawn badly and printed cheaply. They cost five dollars. Of course they're unsigned. So...the buyers carry them to Artists Alley where they ask the actual creator/owner of the character to sign the work, thus giving it real value. When the artist dares to point out that Kabuki does not have one hand larger than the other, or that Cassie Hack would never copulate in such a position with a donkey—yes, it's a sizable industry, depicting superheroes in sexualized ways and then bullying the creator to sign his or her approval—when the creator balks, the shit hits the Comic-Con fan. Hits the metaphoric fan, not the reader.

When the creator refuses to sign the five-dollar knockoff, the collector erupts, accusing the creator of being a selfish prick. A rich, miserly jerk who demands big money for his actual work, prices no working-class fan can afford. Perhaps fueled by shame—yes, they've been fooled into buying a lousy fake, and they're embarrassed to have this pointed out by someone they admire—the would-be collector pitches a fit. The creator who's trying to protect her livelihood as well as the value of the actual work she's sold to others, she's accused and shamed and pilloried in person and online. So not only are you confronted by your Batman having oral sex with your Robin, but you're made out to be the bad guy for not laughing along with the joke and autographing it.

No, none of this is a satisfying answer, but it is a comfort.

For a long time if anyone wanted to buy my books or the books of Salman Rushdie at the Barnes & Noble on Union Square in New York City, they had to ask for the books at the checkout counter. Yes, like cigarettes in a bodega. If left unguarded, my books would be stolen. Salman's would be taken to the public bathrooms and stuffed in the toilets. Barnes & Noble was tired of shoplifters and sick of unblocking clogged toilets so behind the registers the books went.

It helps to know that Edgar Allan Poe's poem "The Raven" was among the most read works of the nineteenth century. It was the *Fifty Shades of Grey* or the *Harry Potter* of its era, but Poe made an estimated $120 from it. That was his initial fee, the only money he got. Unscrupulous printers reproduced the poem endlessly without paying a royalty. Shakespeare also had to contend with stenographers who'd attend his plays, writing down the lines at a feverish pace, and selling the pirated plays filled with stenographic errors.

It's this flood of unauthorized Shakespearean works that drove the price down to a penny, according to the book *The Stealth of Nations*. And it's probable that the penny price kept the plays so popular and preserved their author in the public's taste for so many centuries.

Without piracy, William Shakespeare might've been long forgotten.

It seems the late George Romero would agree. A few years back, at ZombieCon in Seattle, I sat down with him. We talked about how American International had distributed his classic *Night of the Living Dead* without putting a copyright statement on prints of the film. It fell immediately into public domain. Anyone with a print could show it without paying a fee. Anyone could copy and sell it. In the early years of VHS tapes it was the top-selling film because no royalties were due. Romero never saw another nickel from his black-and-white masterpiece.

In retrospect, he wasn't unhappy. The copyright loss had kept the film in constant circulation. Between its initial theatrical release and its jump to videotapes, it was always being shown somewhere as a midnight movie. It had made enough money to cover production costs, he told me. And the film's continuous popularity made Romero a lasting celebrity. It gave him a reputation that attracted financing for his subsequent projects. He shrugged off the loss of the copyright. If the film hadn't exploded in the public domain, he might've been a one-shot director. What looked like a disaster at the time might actually have saved his career.

Mapmakers, cartographers, create fake towns on the maps they make. Then if they find a map published by a different source, but featuring the same fake town, they know it's a copy and can take legal action. With this in mind, you can plant a unique name or phrase that when searched will turn up every site on the web where your work is available. One click, and you've found all the illegal copies. The legendary writer Parker Hellbaby advised me of this trick.

That might not be the answer you want, but if you were my student I'd tell you that's as good as it gets for now.

A Postcard from the Tour

The last man is always a wild card. He loiters all evening as the book signing line stretches, zigzags, dwindles. He might disappear from sight, but he's never gone. The booksellers will step up and ask if he's looking for anything in particular, but he'll wave them off. He's just browsing, he'll say. The garden variety will carry a manuscript in his backpack. Ever since the Art Buchwald lawsuit over *Coming to America*—look it up—we're all terrified of touching a manuscript. The especially nervous writer will bring a box and place it an arm's length away. Then as the manuscript is presented, the writer will feign excitement and ask the last man to put his "gift" into the box. When everyone's gone, the touring writer will ask the store to throw the box in the garbage. Everyone's a witness to testify that the writer never touched the unsolicited work.

It was Doug Coupland, author of *Generation X* and so many other good books, who told me about hotel armoires.

In the days before flat-screen televisions, hotel televisions were hidden inside fake armoires. It was such a hotel cliché that my agent once told me that "armoire" was the French word for "place to hide the television." Coupland clued me in to their other secret purpose. The cabinets never reach the ceiling, but they're too tall for most hotel maids to bother cleaning the tops. Consequently, every author on tour, given manuscripts and self-published memoirs and anything too big or too heavy to lug inside a suitcase for the next few weeks, all these well-intentioned gifts, the writer leaves them hidden on top of the room's armoire. A kinder fate than putting them in the trash.

At Coupland's urging, I started to check atop armoires. Coated with dust, there they were. Expensive art books. Hand-knit sweaters. Beautiful things inscribed to the most famous names in literature, abandoned to the Sargasso Sea of book tours. Like the cobwebbed contents of a pharaoh's tomb.

Other times, the Last Man in Line delivers something less innocuous.

In Portland, as the line ended at the First Congregationalist Church, a young man stepped up and began to deal out Polaroid pictures. He tossed them down on the table in front of me, mostly pictures of old men sleeping. Some were women, young but haggard. They all posed, eyes closed, slumped sideways with their heads pressed against white-painted plywood. He explained that he worked at a popular adult bookstore. They kept a Polaroid camera ready to snap pictures of people they'd ban from the premises. As an example, he tossed down a Polaroid of a smiling thirty-something man wearing a windbreaker. Written in Sharpie below his smile was THE TASTER.

The Taster looked like half the software engineers and game designers I knew. He could've been my letter carrier or a branch manager at a bank.

He was banned, the Last Man explained, because the clerks were always finding him on his hands and knees licking the floor in the porn arcade.

Kid… don't say that I didn't warn you.

I asked, "But what about these sleeping people?" Referring to the old men and young women slumped with their eyes closed.

"They're not asleep," the Last Man in Line told me. "At shift change, we have to go back and check all the movie booths in the arcade, and when I find them I take their picture." He added, "Before I call an ambulance."

On closer inspection, they looked pale. Their faces hung slack. The white plywood was a wall or partition they'd fallen sideways against.

He said, "They're dead." Old men who'd suffered heart attacks or strokes while masturbating. Or they were female sex workers who'd sat in a porn booth to shoot up and had overdosed. There were so many that he'd begun to arrange them in rows across the long table. A gallery in Los Angeles had invited him to hang them in a show, he told me with pride. Arranged on the wall in a single eye-level row, they'd soon encircle a gallery space.

Tours and tours after that night I spoke at a Chapters

bookstore in Toronto. I told about the Polaroids, and a young woman in the crowd shouted out, "Is that the Fantasy store at Northeast Sandy and 32nd?" It was. To the delight of everyone, she shouted, "I *know* that guy. *I was the jism swabber there!*" She was Canadian, she'd explained, working off the books, and it was the only job she could find.

In our incredible shrinking world. For the rest of my life, I'll close my eyes and still see those dead faces.

In San Francisco, the Last Man trailed the line onto the stage at the Castro Theatre. A blond man in a business suit, he seemed so normal. Then he wasn't. His junk was out. He hadn't just opened his fly and hauled it out. In the short time it took me to meet the person before him and sign a book, the Last Man whipped off his clothes, from shoes to necktie. Naked, he berated me, "You think you're so outlandish? Well, autograph this!"

And he flopped his pale, pink tackle on the table.

The Truman Capote story flashed in my head: *No, but I could initial it…* Still, the smile of The Taster is never totally forgotten, and I'd gone skittish. A bookseller once told me of a reader asking for a kiss from the actor Alan Cumming on his tour. The kiss established a precedent like Stephen King's smeared blood, and Cumming had ended up kissing hundreds of readers that night.

I could see this penis going on Instagram, signed by me. Skin is ridiculously difficult to write on, even more so when it's loose, wrinkled penis skin. People forget that writing books is my job, not autographing thousands of penises. I politely declined.

Nothing could've made this Last Man happier. He snapped, "I knew you were a phony." His parting shot.

Which leads us to East Lansing, Michigan, and three high school kids who waited until the book signing line came to an end at one in the morning. My flight out of Detroit was in six hours, and I still needed to get back to my hotel in Ann Arbor, but they pleaded. A friend of theirs had gone out for pizza days before. A drunk driver had T-boned his car, killing the friends he was with and sending him to intensive care in the local hospital. These three asked if I'd stop by, right now at one or two in the morning, and say hello to him.

And no, I won't autograph penises, but I went to the hospital, which was as dim and quiet as any hospital at that hour. The kid had long, black Trent Reznor hair—otherwise he was pretty well wrapped up in plaster and bandages. His mother sat at his bedside. He didn't die; in fact, I saw him on a later tour, grown up. He'd cut his hair.

As I came in and took a seat and started to make small talk with her son, his mom went out in the hallway where I could still hear her crying.

A Couple of Surefire
Strategies for Selling
Books to Americans

If you were my student I'd know what you'd want: a guaranteed formula for success.

That, I would love to give you, but then everyone would use it, and...Chick Lit was such a breakout golden ticket. From *Sex and the City* to *Bridget Jones's Diary*, it sold so reliably publishing switched its terminology. Historically *SF* had meant "science fiction," but after the success of books like *Confessions of a Shopaholic* and *The Devil Wears Prada*, *SF* came to stand for "shopping & fucking." Every hopeful author and editor rushed to market with a pink-covered project, some not as good as the groundbreaking classics, some just plain terrible but hoping to ride the wave, and the flooded Chick Lit market drowned and died.

In short, if I told you a surefire formula, it would fail from overuse.

That said, I will whisper a couple tried-and-true patterns

that American readers always seem to embrace. Let's call these "Tropes for Dopes," shall we?

The first is that the classic American bestseller tends to depict three main characters. One character follows orders, is shy and agreeable, a general all-round good girl or boy. The second character is largely the opposite: a rebel who bullies and breaks the rules, always brashly hogging the spotlight. And the third is quiet, thoughtful, and acts as the narrator, relating the story to the reader.

The passive character commits suicide in some way.

The rebel is executed in some way.

And the thoughtful witness leaves the circumstances of the story, wiser for having seen the fate of the other two characters, and is ready to relay this cautionary tale to the world.

Don't laugh. Arguably the bestselling American books of the twentieth century have followed this formula.

In *Gone with the Wind* the unassuming Melanie Wilkes knows that she'll likely die if she tries to bear a second child. However, as she says so raptly, "But Ashley always did want a big family..." So guess who dies in childbirth? In *Valley of the Dolls* the beautiful, obedient Jennifer North is a showgirl, for the most part a walking piece of lovely scenery who sends her income home to her domineering mother. When breast cancer threatens to change her looks, she takes an overdose of barbiturates. In *Rosemary's Baby*, Terry Gionoffrio leaps from a high window, and the truth-telling Edward Hutchins is murdered by the coven of witches.

Note: Edward "Hutch" Hutchins is also the "gun" of the novel. He's kept alive, off-screen, largely forgotten in a coma, and regains consciousness for a moment to deliver key information before dying. His information sets in motion the discovery process in the third act. A little clumsy, yes, but it plays.

In each case, the suicide of the passive character prompts the execution of the rebel.

Sometimes, not a literal execution. Especially in the case of female characters. Scarlett O'Hara finds herself shunned, an exile despised by her husband, family, and community. Her child is dead, and she's cast out in her despair. Likewise, Neely O'Hara, a fictional character who's named herself after her favorite fictional character (very meta, Ms. J. Susann), also finds herself ostracized. All her husbands have rejected her, as have Hollywood and Broadway. She's a drug- and drink-addled has-been who strove to gain the love of the entire world, but ends up despised by all.

Also consider *The Dead Poets Society*, where the obedient doctor's son shoots himself. The unorthodox teacher is exiled, and the quiet, watchful student is left to testify to both lessons.

In *Cuckoo's Nest* the narrator is mute through much of the book, only watching, then escaping the asylum to tell the tale. Rhett Butler exits the messy lives of the O'Hara clan, returning to Charleston. The witnessing Anne Welles in *Dolls*, so placid and eager to learn, abandons New York for the New England she was trying so hard to escape—at least in the movie. And Nick Carraway leaves the land of Long Island for his own childhood Midwest.

And don't imagine I'd ever pass up such a crowd-pleasing

structure. *Fight Club* might appear to have only two main characters, Tyler and the narrator. But the good-boy narrator still commits suicide. And the bad-boy rebel is still executed. And both acts integrate the two to create the third, the wise witness left to tell us what happened.

The lesson? Don't be too passive. And don't be too pushy. Watch and learn from the extremes of other people. That's our favorite American sermon. And boy howdy does it sell books!

The second sure-shot formula is somewhat more…delicate… to discuss.

Americans are nothing if not voyeuristic. A nation of peeping Toms, we particularly love seeing the misery of other people. Especially if our ogling makes us think we're doing a good deed. And we need to believe that our increased awareness isn't just turning human misery into entertainment, but actually improving the lot of humankind.

Years back, my editor put me in touch with an editor at *Harper's* magazine. That's what a good editor does: try to hook you up with people like Bill Buford and Alice Turner who might offer you reporting assignments or buy your short work, thus increasing your visibility and growing your readership. Thus my editor introduced me to Charis Conn, who edited the "Sojourns" section of *Harper's*. As a faithful member of the Cacophony Society, I was always urban spelunking and Santa Rampaging, and any of these harebrained stunts seemed like good fodder for her section.

At one of our first pitch sessions, Conn warned me, "No

redemptions." Very sternly, she explained that a new chief editor had been hired, and his edict was that no story in the magazine could offer a redemptive ending. I assumed the chief editor to be a cynical curmudgeon. Now my guess is that he was just a savvy judge of what so many Americans want to read.

Take *The Grapes of Wrath*. The Joad family loses their farm. They struggle to migrate west. The oldest generation dies on the journey and are buried ignominiously. They starve and find abuse at the hands of lawmen and deceptive labor brokers. The family falls apart and the next generation is born dead and dropped into a river, not even buried but cast adrift to shame the world.

It's the case made by Horace McCoy in *They Shoot Horses, Don't They?* People are comforted by the misery of other people. And in the late 1960s and the 1970s, with the Vietnam War and Watergate and stagflation and the oil embargo, Americans leaned toward quest stories with a loser ending. I've heard it called "Romantic Fatalism." In movies like *Rocky* and *Saturday Night Fever*, *Midnight Cowboy* and *The Bad News Bears*, people set out confidently toward a goal. They work hard, do their best. And they still lose.

People love to see others suffer and lose. Perhaps this trend toward losers explains the horror vogue in the same period. From *Rosemary's Baby* to *The Omen*, *The Sentinel*, *Burnt Offerings*, and *The Stepford Wives*, we watched innocent people abused and destroyed by sinister forces beyond their awareness.

The formula varies in small ways, but it remains a pornography of someone else's suffering.

Compare 1976's film *Carrie* with 2009's *Precious*. In both an overweight girl (Carrie is fat in the book) in high school lives with an abusive mother. Both girls suffer torment from their classmates. Both have been abandoned by their fathers. Both are bullied into eating—Carrie White's mother telling her to eat and that the pimples caused by cake are God's way of chastising her—Precious's mother just telling her to eat, period.

The biggest difference between the two stories is that Carrie White practices a special power that allows her to eventually slaughter her tormenters. Including her mother. And the stress of doing so causes Carrie's heart to fail.

As for Precious…She's impregnated by her father, twice, gives birth to a Down syndrome daughter, is beaten by her mother, taunted, infected with HIV, she's humiliated and vomits fried chicken in a trash can, but her special power? She learns to read.

Important Note: To sell an extra hundred thousand books, depict a white person teaching a black person how to read. White people who love to read think everyone should love to read. Plus it flatters readers to show them a character who can't read. It's the ultimate way to make your reader feel superior and thus to sympathize with a character. Best of all, it validates reading as a pastime. Whether it's the movie *Fame* or *Driving Miss Daisy* or *The Color Purple*, teaching a black person to read is a plot device that never, ever gets old.

So if you were my student I'd tell you to make a sympathetic character suffer, then suffer more, then suffer worse, never make the reader feel complicit with the tormenters, then—the end. No redemption. People love those books.

Then I'd tell you the opposite. Don't perpetuate the status quo. Let Nick Carraway shout "You're a bag of dicks!" at Tom and Daisy, and "Daisy slaughtered Myrtle!" Let Jay Gatsby leap from his pool and grab the gun. What is our preoccupation with defeat? Why do high-art narratives end poorly? Is it the destruction of the Greek comedies and the Christian church's obsession with tragedy? If more writers strove for paradigm-busting resolutions, would there be less suicide and addiction among writers? And readers?

Above all, I'd tell you, do not use death to resolve your story. Your reader must get out of bed tomorrow and go to work. Killing your main character—we're not talking about a second-act sacrifice—is the cheapest form of resolution.

A Postcard from the Tour

Margaret Buschmann was my first. We did it on a Saturday when no one would be around. In a tiny first-floor office at the Freightliner Corporation where we both worked. There was a roll-down screen we could use as a backdrop, and Margaret brought her own camera. It was hot, a hot August afternoon. We'd always joked that if I ever sold a book we'd do it. So we snuck in when the building would be otherwise empty, and we did it.

Margaret took my first author photo.

The pushback was immediate. The year 1995 was still the '80s as far as I was concerned so I wore a striped cotton turtleneck sweater. Picture Mort on the old Bazooka Bubble Gum comics. A thick, ribbed sweater that rolled up to my chin. And I wore it over a black hoodie sweatshirt so that the hood spilled out of the collar of the turtleneck. Did I mention the temperature? Once Margaret had arranged the lights I was sweating buckets.

She kept looking at me and asking, "Are you sure you want to wear that?"

My haircut, some version of the eighties infamous claw bangs, the sweat stuck the hair flat to my forehead so it needed regular fluffing. I told her I was fine. She said I didn't look very relaxed. We argued.

That rite of passage, the author photo, something I'd anticipated for so long, became an unhappy ordeal. On the book tour for the hardcover of *Fight Club* an interviewer looked at the photo on the dust jacket and asked, "What are you supposed to be? An astronaut?"

A year later for the paperback, my publisher had asked for a different photo. This one a friend snapped in my garden with *Canna* 'Pretoria' blooming in the background. Instead of a turtleneck, the raised collar of a fleece jacket hid my secret, but we'll come back to that.

The author photo. As a rule it's as banal as an actor's head-shot. But there are exceptions. Think of Truman Capote's provocative photo used on *Other Voices, Other Rooms*. Looking like a male Lolita he reclines on a divan and fixes the camera with a come-hither look. That photo got more attention than the book itself.

A friend, the author Joanna Rose, ran author events at Powell's Books for years. She warned that a too-attractive photo would lead to years of meeting disappointed people. To illustrate, I once appeared at the Galway International Arts Festival. Backstage I glanced through a program guide. One photo left me breathless: a woman with fine, pale features and a wild halo of dark curls. It was the legendary poet Edna O'Brien. I couldn't wait to meet her.

A festival organizer whispered that O'Brien would not be appearing. She added that the photo used in the program had been taken in the 1950s. The real Edna O'Brien would be absent because, as the organizer put it, "She's in London, finally getting her hernia fixed."

To search for images on the web is to risk getting sucked down a *Sunset Boulevard* rabbit hole—as in: "How could she breathe surrounded by so many Norma Desmonds?"

Each image marks a specific time and place. The me with the wire-framed glasses and the ratty tweed blazer was taken in Cologne adjacent to a bridgehead. The one with long hair and a black silk T-shirt (Bill Blass from Ross Dress for Less, seven dollars) was taken by Chris Saunders, who showed up at a Manchester pub where I'd just completed a six-hour book signing. He asked for ten minutes, and my glower is because it was 2:00 a.m., and I was semi-soused and could hardly keep my eyes open and would have to repeat the whole dog-and-pony show the next night in Glasgow.

The author photo is the "reality" that underscores the magic of the fictional work. For a person who does the "labor" of inventing and executing the make-believe, the photo is the staid, clear-eyed proof of their professionalism. It's as if an adult version of our annual school photos, this posed, stylized us, will convince readers that writing is a real job. The photo is the equivalent of the actor taking his bow. A performer breaking character, even better, removing his wig or prosthetic nose and breaking the fourth wall to face the audience and prove his humanity. And by creating that contrast, prove his gift. Again, the "real" thing seems intended to highlight the quality of the preceding "fake" thing.

"Yes," the photo seems to insist, "all of the dragons and gorgons and whatnot came from the imagination of this fairly ordinary-looking person!" This photo so interchangeable with that of any realtor in the world.

Perhaps that's why the photos themselves are so unremarkable. No one wants to upstage his own imagination. Plus, of course, a single photo used for years, on many different books, is a branding device. We love our Emily Dickinson tote bags and John Grisham coffee mugs, and those images identify us to like-minded readers.

Not to mention that the photos themselves become a commodity... On one book tour my schedule was dominated by appointments with a different photographer every half hour. I'd be shot by one while the next two or three waited. Each one had his own setups within a short walk. I asked one man what publication his photos were for. He shook his head. There was no specific magazine or newspaper for these photos. He said, "Getty Images is buying a lot of you right now." Meaning, my publisher was sort of renting me by the half hour to speculative shutterbugs, all of whom hoped to get a few images they could sell to the world's largest library of images. This was helping to underwrite the cost of the travel.

For *Vogue Homme* I lay across broken mirrors on the oily

concrete floor of a parking garage while a Russian art director stood next to the photographer repeating, "There! That's the picture! That's the picture!"

In England, a photographer told me not to smile. We were working in the Brighton Corn Exchange, a huge, dim warehouse of a building. I kept smiling, and he kept telling me not to smile. At last I asked why.

"Because," he told me, "you look stupid when you smile."

Enough said. I stopped smiling.

After the Chris Saunders picture in the Manchester pub, I cut my hair. That called for a new author photo so my sister snapped one of me, outside on her deck. If you see a few pine needles in the background, it's the photo in question. This one lasted me for years. It's as banal as banal gets. The archetypal author photo.

Once I started writing comics and coloring books, the author "photo" became a drawing. Pure ego gratification. Once someone who draws superheroes draws your picture, you never want to go back to reality.

Most recently, the Allan Amato photo was a happy medium: a wonderful image, but as staged and retouched as anything between the pages of *Playboy*.

However, life is nothing if not branding and marketing. Packaging and repackaging. And last year my publisher asked for a new photograph. And something snapped.

A friend suggested the photographer Adam Levey, who shoots a lot for Nike. An author photo and a police mug shot, they both struck me as cousins of the infamous "Faces of Meth." I still had the 1995 black hoodie. I hold on to clothes forever. Halloween was coming, and stores were filled with fake tattoos. I shaved my head.

For as long as I've been published I've tried to hide something. My neck. I have a long neck. That's why the turtlenecks and stand-up collars. I gave up. I wondered why an author photo couldn't be ugly. Search the web, and the best prison mug shots are a combination of menacing, tragic, and clownish.

I covered half my neck, my face, and my shaved head with fake tattoos. Adam Levey put on Tom Waits and turned it up, loud. Edna O'Brien, I am not.

Go figure, but the publisher loved it. A week later they didn't like it. They say it might even hurt sales. We are currently in negotiations over a new-new jacket photo sans prison tats.

So Why Bother?

T om would tell you that if you're writing "in order to" achieve anything else, then you should not be writing. So if you're writing in order to buy that big house, or win your father's respect, or convince Zelda Sayre to marry you, forget it. There are easier, faster ways to achieve your real goal. But if you want to write because you love to read and write, consider the following payoffs.

WHY: THERAPY

Tom called his approach Dangerous Writing. His idea, as I understood it, was to use writing as a way to explore some unresolved, threatening aspect of your life. Everything you write is a sort of diary. No matter how it appears to diverge from your life, you've still chosen the topic and characters for a reason. In some masked way, whatever you write is still you expressing an aspect of yourself. You're trapped.

You don't have to start with your worst secret. Just something you're helpless to resolve. Case in point, I once had a neighbor. Chances are we've all had this neighbor. Day after day her music would blast; needless to say it was not Bauhaus or something decent, but it was loud. On the one sunny afternoon I chose to mow my lawn—with an electric lawn mower, please note—she would call the city and summon me to a city-mandated neighbor mediation session about the noise I'd made. Other neighbors warned me, she was a little troubled. A couple of times I'd stepped out of the shower to find her face framed in my bathroom window. She'd say hello as I reached for a towel. Spooky.

She loved her house. It was a wonderful house in a great location, and she often told people she'd die there. I couldn't afford to move. So I wrote *Lullaby*, a book about someone dominated by overwhelming memes and unwelcome music. The plot centered on a poem that killed people when read aloud. The problems I couldn't resolve, I exaggerated. Spinning them out to the wildest possible scenario and ultimately resolving them, on paper at least. The process distracted me from the music next door. In fact, I fed off the annoyance. The irritation I felt, I used to fuel the book.

Behavioral psychologists use a technique called "flooding." Also called "prolonged exposure therapy." If you're terrified of spiders, for example, they might put you in a room filled with spiders. You panic at first, but the longer you remain there the less reactive you become. You acclimatize. Your emotions exhaust themselves. And writing *Lullaby* was my way to subject myself to flooding. By the time I submitted the book to my publisher the noise and music were still there, but I hardly noticed them anymore.

The miracle occurred during my book tour. When I got home, the house next door was vacant. Neighbors reported that a moving van had arrived, and the music lover who'd planned to live there until death had moved.

It's spooky, but it works. Once you use a story or novel to explore and exaggerate and exhaust a personal issue, the issue itself seems to vanish. Magic it's not. I'm not promising miracles. But your personal attachment to the topic or situation will keep you engaged and writing despite the lack of another reward, be it money or recognition. That's my interpretation of Tom's philosophy. Call it catharsis or not, use the writing as a tool to mentally resolve what you can't resolve physically. Take your payday up front.

WHY: HARNESS YOUR MONKEY MIND

Do you remember a particular episode of the original *Star Trek* television series? It involved a robot picked up by the crew of the USS *Enterprise*. As a robot it looked more or less like a floating silver box with antennae, and its purpose was to identify flawed forms of life in the universe and to destroy them. In accord with its prime directive the robot was always chasing after crewmembers it deemed imperfect and vaporizing them with a laser, all the while repeating, "Sterilize! Must sterilize!"

To remedy the crisis Captain Kirk asked the robot to compute pi down to its final digit. The task required the robot's full faculties, thus distracting it. Scotty or whoever used the transporter to beam the preoccupied robot outside the ship's hull, and they destroyed it with a photon torpedo. Massacre averted.

We all have that annoying robot in our heads. Buddhists call it "the monkey mind" and it never rests. The monkey mind is always fretting and chattering, distracting us and driving us nuts. It can't be silenced, so why not do what Captain Kirk did?

Give the monkey mind a big arbitrary task that will keep it busy. By inventing a fictional crisis, you're asking the robot to compute pi to the last digit. And not only does the monkey mind have to resolve the problem, it's also required to create and develop the problem. When you harness that chattering, problem-solving little voice in your head, a strange sense of peace takes over your life.

If you're a worrier, writing can make your nervous anxiety into an asset.

WHY: THE LITTLE-BIG STUFF

The Pacific Northwest of the United States is lousy with beavers. Beavers denuding watersheds. Beavers gnawing down newly planted saplings. This is a century after trappers had driven the beaver almost to extinction in order to supply pelts for beaver-fur hats. What saved the beaver? Not an animal rights campaign or protests. No endangered species litigation. No, what rescued the local beavers was a shift in fashion.

Silk hats came into style. Beaver became passé. Here's just one example of how a seemingly foppish, silly change in the narrative—Nobody wears beaver anymore!—can model a new way of being. Fiction can offer a new way to live, with new goals and values that serve readers better than what's currently in place.

WHY: THE BIG-BIG STUFF

A friend of mine told me about his father dying. My friend sat at his father's deathbed with a tape recorder and prompted him to tell old family stories for posterity. Near the end, it was just the two of them and the tape recorder, my friend Rick coaxing his dad to keep talking. A point came when his father paused and said, "I know you want more stories, but I need to see what Charlie wants."

He said his brother Charlie, Rick's uncle, had been standing in the corner of the room waiting patiently for some time. Of course, to Rick the corner in question looked empty. It was only Rick and his father in the room. Plus, his uncle had been dead a long time. He waited as his father bid Charlie hello and asked his business. And at that point Rick's father, without another word, closed his eyes and died.

The scene is recorded, but Rick has never had the nerve to rewind and listen to the tape.

I love to tell that anecdote because it attracts stories so similar. Lisa tells of her brother's deathbed, where his dog began to howl at the moment of his demise. The dog fell silent, but gazed upward at something, then turned and seemed to follow this something, always gazing up at the ceiling, through room after room until the dog reached the open back door. There the dog stood on the porch and stared as if following the path of something into the sky.

In school I took Ecstasy with some friends and went out clubbing in Vancouver, British Columbia. This was pre–World's Fair Vancouver, when it was cheap, and flophouse hotels lined Granville Street. We were a bunch of kids too buzzed to sleep, sitting around a dark hotel room, each telling about the strangest things that had happened in his life so far. A friend, Franz, whom I hadn't met until my junior year, talked about the summer his parents had sent him to work for family friends. He'd lived in Butte, Montana, but they sent him four hundred miles west to work at a florist shop. He lived with the owners, and one morning before dawn they loaded a fleet of vans with flowers and took off into the dark.

They drove into the desert, a wasteland of sand and sagebrush, until they arrived at an isolated railroad siding. No train, just train tracks that appeared out of the darkness. They waited. As dawn lit up the horizon an Amtrak passenger train appeared. It stopped beside their vans, and Franz's boss instructed his crew to decorate the train. They draped swags of flowers down the sides of the railcars and hung wreaths of flowers on the locomotive. The passengers were bleary-eyed and grousing about the delay, shouting complaints that Franz could only answer with a shrug.

By now a caravan of automobiles had arrived. A bagpipe player climbed to the top of the locomotive and began to play, there in the first light of day, sand in every direction. In that desert cold that people forget is the flip side to the day's sweltering heat. A bride emerged from another car, as did a groom, a wedding party. Franz distributed the bouquets and boutonnieres. The wedding party clambered up onto the locomotive along with a minister and joined the bagpipe player, and a wedding took place.

The moment the bride and groom kissed, Franz and his team began to strip the train of flowers. The newlyweds drove off. The caravan followed, and the train got under way for St. Louis.

Hearing this story among my stoned friends in a fleabag hotel, I was astounded. It wasn't just the Ecstasy, but I thought Franz was pranking me, big time. The wedding he'd described had taken place a decade before, and I'd only known Franz for the past few months. I knew the date of the wedding because I'd been there. It had been my father's second wedding, and he'd been determined to make it a stunt to annoy my mother who hadn't remarried since their divorce. I'd been a kid in a denim leisure suit—look it up—and a kid-aged Franz had pinned the white rosebud to my lapel with the scream of bagpipes filling the vast, flat, freezing-cold landscape.

So many years and miles later, he'd be among my best friends at the University of Oregon. What were the chances? This isn't only my story. It's the bait or seed I use to coax ever more astonishing stories from people.

This is another reason to bother collecting stories. Because our existence is a constant flow of the impossible, the implausible, the coincidental. And what we see on television and in films must always be diluted to make it "believable." We're trained to live in constant denial of the miraculous. And it's only by telling our stories that we get any sense of how extraordinary human existence actually can be.

To shut yourself off from these stories is to accept the banal version of reality that's always used to frame advertisements for miracle wrinkle creams and miracle diet pills. It's as if we've denied the real magic of life so that we can sell each other the sham magic of consumer products. Another example of the shop replacing the church.

If you were my student I'd tell you to reject the "believable" and go looking for the actual wonders that surround you. I'd tell you to read "The Harvest" by Amy Hempel and discover all the truth she deemed too fantastic for the reader to accept.

I'd urge you not to use fiction as a vehicle for social engineering. Readers don't need to be fixed or repaired. Instead, I'd remind you of Tom Spanbauer's directive: *Write about the moment after which everything was different.*

A Postcard from the Tour

His coat wasn't a coat you'd normally see at the Dollar Tree. That's why I saw it. First in aisle seven at Candles, he appeared again in aisle four at Bath Products, the young man wearing a coat with a stand-up collar, like a little fence, like a wall around his neck. That and the length, a Dr. Zhivago length, hitting his legs below the knee. Then this coat walked around to aisle nine and stood at Household Fasteners. When it showed up in aisle eleven at Gift Wrap, then, then it had to be following me.

It's a wonderful warm feeling, being watched and pretending you're not aware of the attention. Being stalked, but in a nice way. It's the opposite of being a suspected shoplifter, and I've had that feeling, too. Plenty of times. No, when you're a public figure the feeling is like when you're a little kid, demanding, "Mom, watch me! Mom, are you watching?" The eyes on you are a validation. They turn any ordinary errand—to buy a ribbon and a box to wrap a birthday present—into a graceful performance.

It used to be different. If a television interviewer needed B-roll footage. Told me to relax and walk casually across some grassy lawn, for example, my every step faltered. My arms flailed.

Anymore, the greedy, attention-whore part of me soaks up the spotlight. It bestows upon me a noble calm. Even at the Dollar Tree.

The remarkable coat stood just at the edge of my vision.

We all want to be pursued. The way every dog tries to get chased by other dogs at off-leash. Now the coat's getting bigger until he's standing at my elbow. My mouth prepares something gracious to say. Something self-effacing, maybe with dulcet tones of gratitude. These encounters always feel like you're accepting an Academy Award.

One time, this one time in Barcelona with David Sedaris, I complained that I never knew what to say to readers who approached me. And Sedaris looked at me and shrugged. "Don't say anything," he told me. "You've shared so much with them through writing. When you meet a reader, it's your turn to listen."

I prepared myself for the shower of accolades. The gushing.

"Mr. Palahniuk?" The coat guy. Young. Shorter than me. "I was at your reading at Broadway Books…"

He had to mean the first time we'd staged the Adult Bedtime Stories. We being Monica Drake, Chelsea Cain, Lidia Yuknavitch, and me. A sold-out crowd had come wearing pajamas and bathrobes as requested. A television station had

David Sedaris

shot a segment as we'd made everyone run a race around the block. For the Broadway Books event I'd ordered cases of oversize stuffed animals. Carnival-big giraffes. Amusement-park-prize big. Lions and white tigers and the like, so big they dwarfed the adults holding them. Chelsea had bought us all bunny slippers. It was a bitch to run down a sidewalk in bunny slippers.

I was listening.

"The day before that reading," the coat guy said, "my brother had died."

I was really listening.

"I was so close to him," the man said. "I was in shock. But I had a ticket. I didn't know what else to do. I just went."

Those words reduced me to nothing but my ears.

"I didn't know how I could go on with my life," he said.

What to say wasn't an issue. All I could do was listen.

"I was standing there," the man said, "and you gave me a giant stuffed penguin." He smiled. "Then I saw that life still had some surprises left. Good things could still happen to me."

Tom always told us, "Write about the moment after which everything is different."

Our lives are saved by such ridiculous moments. Language isn't any help. Especially the words part.

Maybe we shook hands then. Who knows? I'm sure we shook hands. A transcendent moment was taking place in the Dollar Tree. Instead of being starry-eyed and tongue-tied, this stranger was the gracious one. I sputtered and stammered. My throat, go figure, but my throat had gotten so tight. I needed to say something. I stood in shock.

He'd stolen my part.

"Language," as Tom always taught us, "is our second language."

The young man was about to walk away. Then he was walking away, aisle ten, aisle nine.

I called after him. I wanted to say, "Thank you."

You have to talk, otherwise your head turns into a cemetery.

I called out, "That is a great coat!"

Reading List: Fiction

In the first writing workshop I attended we were required to read John Gardner's *The Art of Fiction*, which we never discussed or referred to in any way. Thank God. Its constant references to classic literature were lost on me. I've found that most writers fall into one of two camps. The first rise from academia and write gorgeous stuff with very little plot momentum or drive. The second camp of writers emerge from journalism and use simple, clear language to tell stories rich in action and tension.

My degree is in journalism. My method, journalistic. Instead of reading John Donne I was reading Jacqueline Susann. More people are well read in a lowbrow way, and I wanted this book to appeal to people swamped by books such as Gardner's. Likewise, the fiction I suggest here will be mostly story collections and short novels. It's easier to reverse-engineer short fiction. You can hold the total story in your mind and discover the purpose of every word.

In alphabetical order, they are:

Airships by Barry Hannah
Campfires of the Dead by Peter Christopher
Cathedral by Raymond Carver
Drown by Junot Díaz
Faraway Places by Tom Spanbauer
Generation X: Tales for an Accelerated Culture by
    Douglas Coupland
Heartburn by Nora Ephron
Honored Guest: Stories by Joy Williams
Jesus' Son by Denis Johnson
Miles from Nowhere by Nami Mun
Slaves of New York by Tama Janowitz
The Acid House by Irvine Welsh
The Collected Stories of Amy Hempel by Amy Hempel
The Folly of Loving Life by Monica Drake
The Ice at the Bottom of the World: Stories by Mark
    Richard
The Informers by Bret Easton Ellis
The Night in Question: Stories by Tobias Wolff
The Pugilist at Rest: Stories by Thom Jones
Through the Safety Net: Stories by Charles Baxter

A Postcard from the Tour

It was David Scholl who showed me the future. As proof of how small the world is, I'd known David in Portland where he'd been roommates with friends who'd thrown me my first—and I hope last—surprise birthday party. Dave had been among the seven partners who'd originally opened the restaurant Wild Abandon, insisting the plates should be white when other partners wanted to use an eclectic mix of plates and cups from Goodwill. The business had almost closed after failing to withhold enough for payroll taxes. When we'd first met I hadn't put pen to paper much less joined a writing workshop. Later I'd be an author on tour, and David Scholl would be an executive who traveled the world opening new branches of the Borders bookstore chain. He would be living in Ypsilanti, and when my tour took me through Ann Arbor he would show up for old times' sake.

Borders asked me to shoot a short video that consisted of browsing through a store and touting the books I recommended as good reads for the upcoming summer. I made them a counteroffer. Instead, I'd pretend to be making a training video about how to prevent "stock shrinkage." Doing so, I'd select books and tell the camera each was so good it would be a likely target for thieves. Then I'd pretend to shoplift by stuffing the book down my pants, and move on to the next recommendation.

Our tagline was: "Do you have *Jesus' Son* in your pants, or are you just happy to see me?" Dave and I worked it out, and afterward he showed me the future.

By this he meant the prototype for the new chain of space-age bookstores Borders would soon be building. This first, full-size mock-up stood in the suburbs, a drive from the original brick Borders in downtown Ann Arbor. The new store would occupy maybe one-eighth the total footprint of a current big-box store. He took me inside a single room, not much larger than a 7-Eleven. A couple of walls held shelves of the current bestsellers, but no other books were present. Instead, a large machine, like an oversize photocopier, would print any book a customer might want. It would be bound in a cover of the customer's choice. All within a few minutes.

Maybe half of the store's floor space was dedicated to author appearances. It was all very wood-paneled and carpeted. Rows of chairs faced a screen. Beneath the screen was a sort of built-in desk. "It's for the LongPen system," he explained. This was the brainchild of Margaret Atwood, who didn't want to tour herself into the grave but did want to interact with readers. The way it worked, Atwood—or any writer— could sit at home and present her work to an audience at the store in real time. A camera mounted above the screen would relay the audience to Atwood's monitor. She could answer questions, read selections. Best of all, and here's the pen part of LongPen, readers could align their books on this fixed desk and the author could inscribe and sign long-distance.

Atwood or whoever would hold a computer stylus. At Borders a computer-guided pen would descend to the book. Atwood would write whatever, and the system would direct the pen to inscribe and autograph the book.

A video of the reader-author interaction would be archived online for the reader to later download and keep as a souvenir.

The major hurdle, Dave explained, was convincing the world's authorities on autographs that this remote-controlled signature would constitute an actual, legal autograph. The convincing had taken a few years, but LongPen was finally ruled to be a real autograph. Borders was about to revolutionize the author event.

In these right-size stores around the world authors would be appearing on screens and computers would be signing books. The print-on-demand machine would eliminate the hassles of shipping and stocking books. And Margaret Atwood could stay home in Toronto and not have to drag herself around the world. Dave was justifiably proud. The future was so bright.

And then Borders collapsed.

And then we lost Dave to pancreatic cancer. The problem with loving so many people is that you lose so many.

To Margaret Atwood, I'll continue to look for you on the

road. May your investment in LongPen someday pan out. To date its success has been, for the most part, limited to allowing convicted criminals to do author appearances from prison.

Bless you, David Scholl, may one of your many, many graves always be inside my head.

Reading List: Nonfiction

Be forewarned. I was asked to read at a charity dinner and read the story "Romance" and noticed how one man seated at one table among many tables of well-dressed donors, this man was laughing very hard at the story, particularly at a sad joke about cancer. Go figure, but when I was shown to my seat, it was at this same man's table. As our salads arrived he described his flight arriving earlier that afternoon. As they'd begun their descent into the Portland airport he'd been drinking a glass of wine while a very chatty woman beside him had said how much she loved wine. She'd loved wine all of her life. She'd enjoyed at least a glass of wine every evening until a few months before. Even back then the smallest sip of wine had begun to burn her throat. Soon the pain was so intense she'd given up drinking altogether. Wine, beer, liquor, it all burned her throat. So…she'd decided that God no longer wanted her to drink alcohol, and that was fine so long as that's what

God wanted. Eyeing the man's glass of wine, she told him she still wished she could drink.

The man at the charity dinner was loud and knew how to work a story. Such people are worth studying. Even if the story doesn't pan out, you can still pick up tricks in pacing and voice. I listened.

In response to the chatty seatmate on the airplane he'd finished the last of his wine. He'd explained that he was an oncologist who specialized in rare cancers. What she'd just described to him—that burning sensation when she drank alcohol—was what cancer doctors call "a canary indicator." It was an early and unmistakable sign that she'd developed Hodgkin's lymphoma. He'd advised her to call her lawyer as soon as the plane landed. Her lawyer, not her doctor, because if the symptoms had begun so long ago she had only a few weeks left to live. She needed to write her will and arrange for her funeral.

He told us that the woman was a lot less chatty after that. He gave her his card, and a day later her primary care physician called him to say, "You're right. She'll be dead soon. But you could've been a little less of a prick in the way you told her..."

That's how fast a piece of information can change your perception forever. For the rest of your life, your first sip of alcohol will be about as pleasant as having a biopsy taken. But your second sip—it will taste better than any second sip has ever tasted. That second sip will taste like good health.

The following books will have a similar effect. They will spoil some default part of your thinking, but they will give you a greater appreciation of something you've heretofore taken for granted.

Death in Yellowstone by Lee Whittlesey

Forbidden Words: Taboo and the Censoring of Language by Keith Allan and Kate Burridge

From Ritual to Theater: The Human Seriousness of Play by Victor Turner

Hard Core: Power, Pleasure, and the "Frenzy of the Visible" by Linda Williams

MFA vs. NYC edited by Chad Harbach

Page Fright: Foibles and Fetishes of Famous Writers by Harry Bruce

The Gift by Lewis Hyde

The Program Era by Mark McGurl

The Rites of Passage by Arnold van Gennep

The Ritual Process: Structure and Anti-Structure by Victor Turner

The Sovereign Outsider: 19th Century American Literature, (Non-) Discursive Formation and Post-anarchist Politics by Mathias Hagen König

Trickster Makes This World by Lewis Hyde

Another Postcard
from the Tour

Every so often I ask myself, "Is this where you stop?" I avoid reading reviews because, good or bad, they mess with my head. Triggering mania or depression. But every so often someone brings one to me, laying the best or worst at my feet. The day Salon posted its response to my book *Diary*, I asked myself, "Is this where you stop?"

Teaching is always an option. God bless my parents, but when I quit my last real job, at the Freightliner Corporation, where I mostly loved my work and my co-workers for thirteen years, my mother and father insisted I take a withdrawal from the union instead of quitting full out. So I'm still a member in good standing with the autoworkers' union, with the laminated card to prove it. Writing is a blast, a career beyond anything I'd ever imagined as a kid. But shit happens.

Bad shit, beyond anything even a writer can imagine.

My publisher told me to never tell the story about what went on in San Diego. They promised to provide bodyguards after it happened, and for a while I'd be flanked by security guys who'd whisk me out of stores and into a waiting car the moment a book event was over.

And over the past decade-plus I've tried to unpack the San Diego mess. To tweeze out my responsibility in the disaster.

Maybe I showed too much belly. San Diego, I say here, but really it was in El Cajon. But who knows El Cajon? The bookstore in question had hosted Dr. Laura Schlessinger shortly before me, back when Dr. Laura was still a thing. The manager kept telling me, "You've got more people than Dr. Laura." Who'd gotten eight hundred people. In a big store in a shopping center of big-box stores, still daylight, I had to stand in the center of everyone and turn a little to see them all.

Not a couple of words into my blather, I could see people at the edge of the crowd. Certain persons, spaced at more or less equal distance apart, held up large sheets of poster board. The boards were fluorescent hot pink, pale blue, pale green. The people held them in both hands, overhead. They'd written something on these signs, and they kept turning in place, slowly, displaying the messages. Each time I risked looking, a particular sign was turned the wrong way. Was I reading? Answering questions? I forget, but I was giving people these heavy gilded crowns as reward for asking things. Different colors of glass jewels ran around the outside of the crowns, and white satin padded the inside. This was a couple dozen big crowns I'd shipped to the store beforehand. I'd autographed the satin. I thought they looked snazzy.

Between doing something and saying something, I caught sight of a neon poster board sign. It read: DID YOU KNOW

THAT CHUCK PALAHNIUK RAPED AND KILLED A NINE-YEAR-OLD BLACK GIRL IN 1987?

This wasn't just one sign. All the signs held aloft, turning slowly, stationed throughout the bookstore...they all made that claim.

A tricky situation, to say the least. I felt too shocked to take offense. It occurred as some prank. After years watching the Cacophony Society prank whole cities. Like doctoring an Apple billboard that showed a huge close-up of Amelia Earhart so that it read, "Think Doomed." Or one Easter morning staging a passion play and crucifying a gigantic stuffed pink Easter bunny on a telephone pole immediately outside the front doors of a packed Baptist church. I knew that sometimes pranks can go too far and fall flat, and I didn't want to harsh on these young aspiring pranksters.

No, I've never raped or murdered anyone, black or white, just to settle that question. So I did a callout to the sign holders and asked them to stow the signs, and they did. The event moved on, and someone...somebody asked me what I'd never bring myself to depict in fiction.

My response has always been the same. I'd never depict the senseless torture and killing of an animal. Even in make-believe. The scene in David Foster Wallace's *Girl with Curious Hair* where the characters douse the little puppy with lighter fluid and set it on fire and laugh as it runs around a basement screaming until it dies...that had done a number on me. Consensual violence I can get behind, hence *Fight Club* with all of its structure and rules. But the moment that novel's characters veered into attacking someone—the mayor's special envoy on recycling—and the moment we see Marla's black eye, that's when I stopped liking the story and could happily bring it to an end.

So I gave my speech about consent and about animals being innocent victims of everything. I showed belly. I showed my belly to the crowd. Then I showed too much belly by reciting a John Irving poem about a beloved dog. Old and dying, the dog was so obedient that as it died and began to lose control of its bowels it painfully dragged its dying self onto a spread-out patch of newspapers so it wouldn't soil the carpet. And there it died.

By then I was on my back, showing full belly in public. That poem kills me, as does Amy Hempel's essay "A Full Service Shelter," written about the volunteer work she does in Manhattan animal shelters. There she describes, as a cost-cutting measure, how each doomed dog is given its lethal injection of phenobarbital in full sight of the heap of dead dogs. The dying dog is dragged by a leash and forced to climb this soft, still-warm heap of dead animals, so that it will die on the pinnacle, atop the previous dog that's barely died, and all of this brutality is shelter policy because it prevents the risk of back injury to any employee who'd otherwise be forced to lift and carry any fully dead animal.

Fuck me. I was stupid. I showed full belly, something no one onstage is supposed to do. Instead of making the emotion occur in my audience I got myself choked up. With all this talk about the suffering of poor beasts, I'd gotten misty-eyed and tight throated. A self-indulgent, cardinal no-no for the writer of *Fight Club*.

My point is that I can own what happened. I called down the bad mojo on myself.

The blah-blah presentation ended, and the book signing began. With such a big turnout the store's staff had to run the registers. I sat alone in a back corner, and a line of patient readers queued up to say hello. Among them was the group who'd brought the rape/murder signs. I asked about their motive, and they seemed sheepishly to say they thought it would be funny in a Project Mayhem way. A prank. No point in shaming them. Shit like this happens when you're pushing the envelope. I've pulled some boneheaded moments, too, told some cheap-shot jokes and been booed by vast crowds. We shook hands.

One among them gave me a book to sign. A shaggy blond beach type, maybe he was a surfer? He looked like a surfer. A surfer or a skater, he stepped forward like their leader and gave me a novel by Don DeLillo.

The book's cover was defaced with scribbles and hash marks in thick black felt-tipped pen, but it was still a DeLillo book. People bring me all kinds of books to sign. Usually Bibles. Usually they ask me to write "I suck Satan's cock" in their family Bible and to sign it. More than a handful of these Bibles looked to be ancient, bound in leather and gilded, with Dore illustrations and faded family genealogies, so elegant they look positively Gutenberg. And I always give a polite no. A handshake follows. There's no game in embarrassing anyone.

As usual, I said I didn't sign books by other authors.

And the blond said, "This is one of your books."

This is while hundreds of people wait in a line that snakes up and down the aisles of bookshelves.

I point out that Don DeLillo's name is on the cover.

The guy insists I sign. I don't sign. The surfer and his crew of pranksters depart. No big deal.

It can occur as a tragedy, to meet a writer. Physical proof of the author means you'll never meet the characters you've come to accept as friends or heroes. I've experienced this so many times that I avoid meeting people whose work I enjoy. And understanding this disappointment, I try to control the damage.

Me, the faggoty, animal-loving, poetry-spouting, choked-up writer who turned out not to be the living embodiment of Tyler Durden, I got back to meeting people and signing books. People step up to the table with such excitement, it's impossible not to try and match it smile for smile. Hug for hug. Some readers have hyped themselves almost to tears. The quiet people have to be coaxed to say hello. Pictures have to be posed for. I ask questions and listen for key words I can mimic in funny inscriptions. A person is meeting me for the first time, and I try to meet each as if he or she is the only person I'm meeting that evening. This leaves no attention for anything beyond the little bubble of me and the person to meet next.

For years my longest signing had been at Barbara's Bookstore in Oak Park, Illinois. Eight hours. Torture at the time. Now eight hours would be light duty. My book signings regularly stretch to twelve and fourteen hours. David Sedaris signs books until after four in the morning. Stephen King will sign only three or four hundred items and bookstores hold a lottery to choose the lucky readers.

Do you see what I've done here? I've shifted to big voice, describing similar events in a general way to suggest time passing that night in El Cajon. One person I do remember, a mom came forward in line to thank me. I'd made presents and sent them to her teenage son and daughter. At first she seemed angry, but she was actually a little speechless that a stranger would do something that would make her children so happy.

She hadn't stepped away a moment before the fire alarms began to wail. Something soft struck me on the chest. Soft thuds pelted down on the signing table and on the carpet around me. With that backdrop of loud sirens, only the few people at the head of the line could see what had happened. Most of the line snaked into the distance. The store staff was busy, far away, at the cash registers.

People who witnessed the evening have since created an online discussion thread. They report that the blond young man—the prankster with the mutilated DeLillo novel—when I'd refused to sign his book he'd left the store with a compatriot, riding a motorcycle. Soon after, the two had come back, parking the motorcycle on the sidewalk directly in front of the store's main doorway. They'd returned carrying a large mailing tube.

According to witnesses, the two men had swung the tube to launch whatever was packed inside it.

White mice had struck me. The mailing tube had been filled with those pink-nosed, red-eyed, little white mice that pet stores sell to feed snakes. These mice hit me. They rained down on the floor and the table with such force. They weren't dead, but they were dying. Their bodies twisting slowly. Their necks and spines, broken on impact. Their legs trembled and blood ran from their mouths. People stood in line, stunned. Sirens wailed.

There was nothing to do but apologize for the delay. No one came to help. I started to gather the mice. In my hands, some arched their backs for the last time, twitched against my palms and died. Some were dead but still warm by the time I found them shattered against bookshelves and scattered down aisles. There were so many. I collected them all and carried them to a stockroom to lie in peace.

The young men who'd thrown them had escaped through the fire exits. That explained the alarms. Fire alarms. Once I'd moved the dead and dying little animals to the back, the store fell quiet. Crowded but silent. Some four hundred people still stood in line, and few had had a clear view of what had taken place. Blood smeared my hands and spotted the signing table. In the bathroom I washed. I went back and finished my job.

According to the witnesses, no one realized what would happen until it was too late. No one could stop the action so they'd descended on the motorcycle and torn it to pieces. No police were called. The men escaped on foot. I'm still in contact with the booksellers, and they tell me the miscreants were locals. On occasion, the blond man still continues to drop into the store. He must be nearing middle age.

Since then I collect stories about blood at author

appearances. Like the time in Seattle where fans bullied Stephen King into smearing his blood in fifteen thousand books. Or the kid at Tower Records who slashed his wrists with a razor blade while standing next to Clive Barker, shouting, "Clive, this is for you!" Or in New Orleans, at the venerated music venue Tipitina's, when a young man fell and fractured his skull during my reading of "Guts," the bookseller later explaining to me that after the decades of punk rock shows and heavy metal mosh pits the club had hosted, a book reading had caused the worst injury the venue had ever seen. That same night Monica Drake had appeared with me, making the crowd laugh so hard that no one noticed when she cut her leg on a piece of stage equipment. We'd all been so jazzed with excitement that none of us noticed how we were slipping around in a puddle of Monica's blood all night.

Such stories are a comfort.

That, and sometimes reader pushback amounts to payback. A good author bullies the reader, when justified. The author's job is to challenge and frighten the reader when necessary, at least to surprise the reader. Often to charm the reader into experiencing something he or she would never voluntarily submit to. It should come as no shock that an offended or bullied reader would seek revenge. There is that.

My publisher advised me never to tell the story about the dead mice. They were afraid of copycats. For a while I got bodyguards. I felt like Bret Easton Ellis.

I asked myself, "Is this where I stop?" Now I've told the story about the mice.

I didn't stop.

Troubleshooting Your Fiction

When I played high school basketball, a coach made me wear ankle weights. These consisted of several pounds of lead buckshot sewn into a leather pouch that fastened with Velcro. Only bell-bottom jeans could hide these fat collars strapped around my ankles, and I wore them from waking until bedtime, every day for months.

Later in life I hired a trainer who made me tie a string around my waist and wear it under my clothes at belly-button height. The ankle weights chafed and made my feet sweat. The string left a red groove by the end of each day. But my legs got stronger, and I learned to always (usually) engage my core muscles.

So if you were my student I'd tell you, yes, someday you can go back to using "is" and "has" verbs, as well as abstract measurements and "thought" verbs. You can occasionally use passive voice and summaries. Eventually you can use the received text of clichés, if appropriate. But first I want you not to. For the next couple of years, at least, I want you to follow the rules of this book. By doing so you'll be forced to invent new ways of telling a story. You'll learn to stay within a scene and move your characters through their world in a physical way. Above all, you'll grow beyond the easy "default" ways of writing that rob your work of its power.

Writing is nothing if not problem solving. These rules that hobble you now will ultimately strengthen your work.

The following is a quick diagnostic check. Find what seems to be your weakness, and consider the possible cause and solution.

Problem:	Your narrative voice is boring.
Consider:	Read it aloud. Do you vary sentence length and construction? Do you balance dialogue with physical action and gesture? Do you mix different textures of communication?
Problem:	You fail to build tension.
Consider:	Have you established a clock? Do you limit and revisit your story elements (settings, characters, objects)? Does introducing new elements force you to use passive verbs such as "is" and "has"? Do you use tennis-match dialogue that instantly settles the tension raised by every question?

	Do you make every series a series of three? For example, "planes, trains, and automobiles" or "the Father, the Son, and the Holy Spirit"? Instead, consider using two or four items in each series. Three items completes too much energy.
	Do you stay within a scene, or do you fall into frequent flashbacks that jolt your reader out of the fictional moment?
	Are you taking things too lightly? Remember, too many comedians and not enough strippers will continually negate any tension that might arise. Add more strippers. Cut back on your cleverness.
Problem:	**Your stories ramble and meander without coming to a climax.**
Consider:	Did you plant a gun? What unresolved expectation can you revisit?
	What character can you kill in the second act in order to heighten the seriousness?
	Can you send your characters on a brief road trip that will wreck their complacency?
Problem:	**You lose interest in the work before it's complete.**

Consider:	Does it explore a deep, unresolved issue of yours? Are you depicting a horizontal series of plot events that doesn't deepen? Are you reintroducing objects and allowing them to morph as symbols?
Problem:	**A scene runs on and on without contributing to the horizontal or the vertical of the story.**
Consider:	Before writing the scene, did you plan its purpose? Does it establish or introduce something? Or does it deepen the risk and tension? Is it a lull to pace an upcoming reveal, or to suggest time passing? Or does it reveal something and resolve tension? Always, always have some inkling of your scene's purpose before you begin to work on it.
Problem:	**Your work fails to attract an agent, editor, or audience.**
Consider:	Does that really matter? If writing is fun...if it exhausts your personal issues...if it puts you in the company of other people who enjoy it...if it allows you to attend parties and share your stories and enjoy the stories told by others...if you're growing and experimenting

	with every draft…if you'd be happy writing for the rest of your life, does your work really need to be validated by others?
Problem:	**Your fiction fails to engage the reader.**
Consider:	Do you rely too much on big voice and abstract verbs? A reader can always be entranced by an object in motion within a setting. The eye moves in tiny jerks unless it's tracking a moving object. Are you clearly depicting an object or person in motion?
Problem:	**Your beginnings don't hook readers.**
Consider:	Do you begin with a thesis sentence that summarizes, or do you begin by raising a compelling question or possibility?
Problem:	**You don't have time to write.**
Consider:	Do you listen to music while commuting, or can you allow yourself to daydream in silence? Do you keep a pad and pen in the bathroom? Beside your bed? In your car? Do you make the most of your writing time by compiling notes and ideas throughout the rest of your life?

Problem:	You don't want to freak out your family.
Consider:	By telling the truth you allow others the same opportunity. So long as you're clearly writing fiction, you force other people to own the fact they might be the characters (and they might be dicks). If they take offense, you can simply deny that any characters are based on them.
Problem:	You can't find a workshop.
Consider:	Start one. Enroll in a class. Find any social structure that will hold you accountable to produce work.
Problem:	Your workshop sucks.
Consider:	As Ken Kesey once told me, "All workshops suck at some point." You will love and hate one another. Ultimately, does your workshop keep you producing work?

Ken Kesey

Problem:	**Writers in your workshop demand major surgery on your work. They suggest useless revisions or state baseless opinions that offer no creative insight.**
Consider:	Screenwriters I know must sit through marathon meetings with producers and actors, all of whom want reasonable and unreasonable changes to the script in question. A good writer knows what she can use and makes note of the helpful advice. And a professional knows not to push back, but just to smile and thank everyone for their contribution.
Problem:	**Your audience isn't surprised by your work.**
Consider:	Are you? Do you withhold your best idea for the end, or can you use that strong idea near the beginning and trust that the story will naturally build to a stronger climax than you ever could've initially imagined?
Problem:	**You write from an outline and lose interest partway to completion.**
Consider:	How about writing from a partial outline? Know the mechanical breakdown at the end of

	the second act, and trust that the story will resolve itself better than you could ever anticipate. How can you surprise your reader if you can't surprise yourself?
Problem:	**Your work fails to break readers' hearts.**
Consider:	Are you being too clever? Have you established emotional heart authority? Does your work sound too much as if it's being told by a writer instead of an actual person?
Problem:	**Your main character is a shallow stereotype.**
Consider:	Can you make her do something totally despicable but for a noble reason?
Problem:	**Your work isn't as good as Amy Hempel's.**
Consider:	No one's is.

A Postcard from the Tour

About the time DVDs first appeared, but before the death of the typewriter, my father called.

By long distance, he asked if I'd spend Christmas with him. He told me to catch the Coast Starlight Limited from Eugene, Oregon, to Portland, then switch trains and ride the Empire Builder as far east as Spokane. A pain, but what a surprise! On Christmas Eve he picked me up at the station. Chains clanked on the tires of snowplows as they crossed and crisscrossed to keep the downtown streets clear.

My father and I, we hadn't spent a holiday together since I was in Cub Scouts. In two terms I'd graduate with an undergraduate degree in journalism and begin paying down a mountain of student loans. Journalism because it looked like a safe bet. Not writing fiction because, geez, everyone knew fiction was a colossal crapshoot. We drove to a truck-stop diner where he drank a cup of coffee while I ate a chicken-fried steak. He carried a thick, brown envelope under one arm and set it on the table between us.

To show me, he lifted the flap. He slid out a thick stack of paper, lined sheets of notebook paper. These he fanned across the table between us. Handwriting covered the pages. Words scribbled in pencil and ballpoint pen.

He said, "You want to make your old man rich, don't you?"

Why was I surprised? This guy, my father, was always holding up a paper clip or the plastic tab used to hold shut the bread bag. He'd say, "The man who invented this never had to work another day in his life!"

He figured he could publish a book and sell it to railroad employees, current and retired. To judge from the union rolls, he said, it would do big business. The handwritten words were sentences were paragraphs were stories he'd collected from co-workers. He'd already promised them a small cut of the profits. To put him on easy street, all I needed to do was edit the material. Maybe doctor the stories a tad, he said. Add color and action, to polish them into rollicking, two-fisted yarns. A *Cannery Row*, but about freight trains. With me as Steinbeck.

And railroad stories…I'd grown up hearing them. He'd bring them home to tell at breakfast. Stories about the whorehouses along A Street in Pasco, just across the tracks from the roundhouse, a short walk for any crew. Or stories about what crewman had a different wife and family at each end of his run. The stories about tribesmen on the Colville Reservation who'd get drunk on foggy nights, to sit on the tracks with a blanket pulled over their heads, to fall asleep and wait. Long descriptions of the bloody guts and the delay. Ghost stories about the same. Tales about rednecks in Idaho who sat trackside and used rifles to blow out the windows of Cadillacs being shipped to Seattle on open-sided car carriers. Picture a hundred showroom-ready Caddies shot to shit. Stories about these same hillbillies causing derailments — with concrete blocks, with iron bars — so they could loot the crushed boxcars. Stories about the yard bulls who beat the teeth out of hobos they'd found hitching rides.

But these stories, the ones he'd brought me, scribbled down by brakemen and freight conductors, these weren't like the ones I'd loved. In blocky handwriting, here were scenes of nice guys playing pinochle around the coal-burning, pot-bellied stoves in old-timey cabooses. No dismembered ghosts or switchyard whores haunted these scrawled notes. If any-thing, these stories needed un-polishing. They didn't teach un-editing in journalism school, but I couldn't say no.

He watched me shuffle the pages. He asked, "You dating anyone?"

By this he meant a girl. When was I going to get married and start a family? By my age he'd been married, had three kids, and had already thrown a bah-zillion track switches for the Northern Pacific. These days he lived by himself in a tiny house deep in the woods on Mount Spokane. While I pretended to read the stories he got up to use the pay phone. Pay phones, like typewriters, were about to disappear from the world, but we hadn't the foggiest idea, not yet.

He came back to the table smiling. He'd been offered a holiday shift that paid triple time. That kind of big money he couldn't turn down. He told me to eat up so he could drop me at a cinder-block motel in the fried chicken-smelling fast-food strip at the edge of downtown. Me and my fat envelope of so many censored recollections without tension or suspense.

"I understand," I lied. Work has always been my family's noble reason to escape itself. We'd volunteer for double shifts on Thanksgiving and Christmas. "I'd love to be there," we'd tell each other, shrugging, "but I'm on the schedule at work."

Typewriter ribbons and landline phones and record players, where did everything go so fast?

My dad went to work.

Cold and alone the next morning, Christmas morning, I turned on the motel television.

A movie was just beginning. A Cat Stevens song played on a record album while an unseen actor lighted a candle. He wrote a suicide note. The actor stepped up on a chair, put his head in a noose. He kicked the chair aside. Over the course of the movie he pretended to cut his throat. To self-immolate. To disembowel himself, and he never died. Instead, he proposed marriage to Ruth Gordon.

What Tom would call, *The moment after which everything is different.*

Would you believe me if I told you that my father bought me my first dictionary? Back in high school when I'd told him I wanted to write he gave it to me for Christmas. God only knows where he'd found it. Decades before the internet, he dragged home a dictionary the size of a suitcase. Glossy full-color plates filled the middle pages, pictures of precious and semiprecious minerals, the animals native to every continent, the leaves and flowers of the world. Its size and weight made it impossible to carry, but it was the biggest and most expensive he could find. May one of his many, many graves always be in my head.

As the movie ends on television, I'm still sitting in that musty motel room on Christmas Day. But the outside world isn't the same world. The snow...even the sky is a new sky.

This world is a world where anything can happen. Downtown Spokane isn't just Spokane, not anymore. And I wander in the maze of these empty, icy streets marveling at the explosion of what's suddenly possible.

Soon after the death of my father, but just before answering machines and disposable cardboard cameras began to disappear, I flew to London. I went on tour for something, some book, making the rounds of radio interviews with different programs on the BBC. In cabs, in the Underground, escorting me was my assigned publicist, Sue. Beautiful Sue, men whistled at her from construction scaffolding. And maybe people stared at Sue, but she was on the lookout for the elephant.

The Sultan's Elephant, it was a piece of street theater. Part robot, part puppet, it was performance art hired by the city. Beginning one morning with what appeared to be a wooden spacecraft crashed into a steaming crater on Pall Mall, the performance was to last seven days. As per rumors, this gigantic robotic elephant would ramble through central London.

No one we met had actually laid eyes on the elephant. Oh, we saw the traffic jams. In every cab we hailed, the driver was cursing the elephant. We'd sit in gridlock, hearing how the elephant was on Gower Street or in Soho Square, always around the next corner, always just out of sight. We heard the car horns honking. The week was dwindling. The Sultan's Elephant would be gone soon. Sue and I were hopeful, but we had a book to promote.

On the elephant's last day in London, we went to the Waterstones bookstore on Piccadilly. A city-block-size building all glass on the outside that booksellers called the Crystal Palace. We shook hands with another writer and spoke to an audience of book buyers in an upper-floor conference room. People ate box lunches. Everyone present kept sneaking looks out the windows. We listened for any chorus of angry honking that might herald the elephant's arrival.

What did we discuss? Was the sun shining? Does it matter?

As we left the building, walking down a concrete stairway to a metal fire exit door, we heard it. Music echoed between the cornices and caryatids, the very wedding cake curlicue pediments and carved-stone Palladian windows of the Charles Dickens office buildings. Sitar music and flutes and drums floated toward us. Cars along the one-way street disappeared as if something beyond the next curve was blocking the flow of traffic. People on the sidewalks forgot to go anywhere. Businessmen wearing hats, carrying umbrellas and briefcases. People pushing strollers. Police officers, beautiful Sue and me, we all stood and watched to see what would appear from around the far bend in the road.

Bankers in pin-striped suits. The stylish yuppies, people in those days used to call Sloane Rangers. The street turned into a still photograph of everybody holding their breath.

A dozen books later, I'd tell this same story at a dinner party. My version of seeing the elephant. I'd be sitting at one end of a long table. At the far end a woman I didn't know, hadn't met, she'd begin to cry. The attention would swing to her and she'd explain between sobs that she'd also been in London that week. She'd seen the elephant and ever since had been trying to tell people the tale. "No one believed me," she would say, struggling for a breath. "No one could understand how it changed me..." She'd begun to doubt her own memory of the event.

Hearing me had confirmed that she wasn't deranged. She hadn't been exaggerating.

There first appeared a team of men wearing turbans and billowing pants, walking in the center of the street. Behind them rose and fell huge gray feet, legs as tall as the buildings, a waving trunk, tusks, and high atop the elephant's back, a temple filled with topless female dancers. More men walked beside the huge feet and trailed behind it. Pent up behind them was the stalled traffic.

The veiled, bare-breasted dancers danced. The musicians played. Crowded faces stared from high-rise windows eye-level with the elephant's jeweled head and the *Arabian Nights* temple fluttering with banners and streamers.

The elephant's trunk swung and let loose with a geyser of water. With the blast of a fire hose it sprayed the crowds. Cold water. People screamed, pushing to find shelter in doorways. Paper shopping bags burst. Screams turned to laughter, everyone's shoes skidding on wet pavement.

Above us, a young man stepped out an open window. He wore a dark-blue shirt of some shiny, satiny fabric and stepped onto the ledge of a gingerbread cornice. Above the elephant's head, he stood suicide-high above the street, using both hands to hold a cardboard camera. He squinted through the viewfinder, clicking pictures, when the trunk swung in his direction. A blast of water struck him, and he dropped the camera. The drums and flutes went quiet. The horns stopped honking.

The group stare of so many people followed that falling camera, down past windows, our eyes tracked it past windows, windows, windows, past staring-out faces until it shattered on the concrete. The young man slipped as well, in his dark-blue shirt and his slick leather shoes, shuffling fast on the wet cornice sloped to shed rain. His hands grabbing at air. No one's scream was their own and mine joined Sue's and our scream blared with the screams of lawyers and topless dancers and screaming cabdrivers as we all saw the man fall.

People turned away. People who'd closed their eyes, they wouldn't look. They were so sure he was smashed dead at our feet.

The moment after which everything is different.

Did I forget to mention the flagpole within grabbing distance? If so, I didn't mention it because the flagpole wasn't there. It wasn't there until the man grabbed it. His hand caught the wet flagpole jutting out from the cornice, and he stopped his falling for the heartbeat it took for people inside the open window to grab his shirt.

We'd watched a man die. He was dead in our minds, and then he wasn't.

He'd been saved. The horns and drums started up. The elephant took another gargantuan step. We shivered in our soggy clothes now. Complained to each other how our shoes and hair were ruined. Our wet wristwatches had stopped. Taxi horns drowned out the music.

Paper cameras and wristwatches and copies of *The Celestine Prophecy*, how could things of such vital importance just evaporate the way they did? That entire world of dot-matrix printers and pulling the tracking strips off the edges of continuous-feed printer paper—gone.

Before the elephant went out of sight people were already telling the story: he was nothing short of Lazarus, this man who fell and came back to life.

Probably they're still telling it.

In the last days of road maps and telephone books, before global positioning systems and ride-sharing apps, my French editor hosted a dinner at her apartment on the Left Bank. As the guest of honor I sat at the head of the table. The other guests were her friends, smoking and drinking and arguing without rancor about who among them had gotten the others addicted to heroin. My impression was that everyone present had been or was currently a dope fiend. An assumption supported by the way they excused themselves from the table in pairs to use the bathroom and returned grinning and stumbling.

Me, I'd arrived from Portland that afternoon, exhausted with jet lag, and had spent the afternoon posing for a photographer who asked me to crouch on the floor in the empty closet of my hotel room because he needed an all-white background. The halo flash he used—a ring-shaped strobe that encircles the camera, meant to light the subject from every angle—he said it would hide the sagging bags and erase the red veins of my tired bloodshot eyes. The next day would be interviews and more photographers, with a book signing in the evening and a long dinner with a table of journalists. And tonight I only wanted to get to my hotel and pass out, but this party was in my honor so here I sat, squinting against the cigarette smoke, not understanding a lick of French and feeling, more and more, like the puppy in chapter 2 of *The Great Gatsby* surrounded by loud drunks, sleepy and ignored.

Did I mention I was angry, too? More than anything I was fuming mad. Tomorrow I'd be expected to work hard, and the least these French people could do was feed me and put me to bed. What's more, my grandmother had died the day before. She'd been taking a medication to blunt the pain of her arthritis so she could keep working, and it had masked the symptoms of acute diverticulitis. My grandmother had died suddenly and painfully, and her funeral would be the next day, and I would miss it because I had a book tour.

To make matters worse, the host set a platter of Brie on the table. As the guest of honor I was expected to take the first slice from the thick wedge of cheese, something they explained to me in English. They were also trying to teach me the French cautionary rhyme, "Red before white and you'll

be all right. White before red and you're better off dead."
Meaning, if you drink white wine before red wine you'll
suffer a hangover. At their urging I repeated the French back
to them. Taking the knife, I cut the smallest bit I could
manage off the pointed tip of the Brie wedge.

The table, the table went nuts. Junkies or not, they all
squawked, "How American!" And, "Just like an American!"
It seems I'd helped myself to the center of the cheese, the
softest, creamiest bit. The correct thing to do would've been
to slice along the entire side of the wedge, taking both a
smidgen of the center as well as a share of the hoary rind.

After my apologies they went back to their argument,
throwing impossible French words at each other. A man and
woman staggered out of the bathroom and began to excuse
themselves. They had to work in the morning and needed to
leave early to get some rest.

Early? It was the middle of the night. I saw my chance and
begged them for a ride. They shrugged. I climbed into the
backseat of their tiny car, and we sped away.

This is how high they were: They'd stop at red lights. The
light would turn green, and they'd stay stopped. The light
would turn red, and they'd stay stopped. Other cars eddied
around us, honking. We'd hurry off, only to stay stopped as
they nodded off at another green light.

My anger was held in check by my fear. I couldn't remember the name of my hotel, much less the address. We kept
driving past the same statues and fountains. We were driving
in circles. Where we were, who knew? I could bail out, but
was this a safe neighborhood or a sketchy one?

At last the lights of the Eiffel Tower loomed ahead of us. The strung-out driver hit the gas, and we sped through one, two, three red lights, racing, weaving through the sparse traffic until the front wheel struck the curb and we bumped to a stop, parked on the sidewalk at the base of the tower...beside a police car.

The man and woman leapt from the front seat and began to run across the plaza, leaving their car doors open, the headlights on, the engine running. The police couldn't miss this. As they ran toward the area beneath the tower, the couple shouted, "Run, Chuck! Run!"

They had drugs. I knew they had drugs. They were evading arrest, leaving me in a car filled with drugs. The police were looking at me, and I was going to a French prison unless I acted fast.

Of course I ran. All the French I could speak was, "*Rouge puis blanc...*" I dashed after the escaping heroin dealers. The police ran after me. We were all running across the plaza, between the legs of the Eiffel Tower.

And there they stopped. The couple stopped, and I stopped. Panting and breathless, they shouted, "Look up, Chuck! Look up!"

A few bystanders stood around. The police officers were catching up.

The couple already had their heads tilted back, gazing skyward. I looked up.

From where we stood, under the center of the tower, it rises upward like a vast, square tube. Floodlights turn the tapering structure into a bright tunnel of light that seems to stretch into infinity. My heart pounding, sweating, a little drunk, I looked up into this glorious, blazing tunnel.

And the entire world disappeared into darkness.

Nothing existed. With no visual points of reference I lost my balance and collapsed to the sticky concrete. Everyone gasping in unison, that and my heartbeat were all I could hear. I was blind. The world was gone. And my fingers clutched at the rough ground for fear I'd lose that, too.

Someone began to clap. Everyone joined the applause.

My eyes adjusted. The druggy couple and the police were still there. The Eiffel Tower rose over us, no longer a tunnel of light, but a looming, dark oil derrick.

Will you think I'm crazy? Worse, will you think I'm a liar if I tell you that during that long moment when the world had disappeared, while I seemed afloat in nothingness, I heard my dead grandmother speak? People invent this stuff, but where does our imagination come from? All I can tell you is what her voice said. It told me, "This is why we're alive. We come to earth to have these adventures."

The moment after which everything is different.

The heroin addicts were only pretending. During the course of the dinner, the entire table had argued over the one experience I had to have, that they had to provide for me, while I was in Paris. Everyone knew I was exhausted, and that my schedule wouldn't allow for any sightseeing. So they'd plotted to bring me to this exact spot at exactly midnight when the lights of the Eiffel Tower would be extinguished. They'd baited me over the cheese, goaded me to frustration. Then they'd kept me awake. Once I was in a car they'd dawdled at traffic lights, always stalling so they could arrive at the Champ de Mars moments before midnight.

The panicked dash had been staged to deliver me breathlessly to this spot. Even the police understood, more or less, what was taking place. I'd been wrong about everything.

These strangers I'd hated so much, in this city I'd begun to fear and despise, they'd all conspired to antagonize me, to enrage me. A team of people had ultimately plotted to bring me to a joy I never could've imagined.

We keep tabs on Tom. Some of us, his former students. Someone will drop by his house and later spread the word as to whether or not he could recall her name. Whether he was losing weight. If he might even be writing again. Eventually every writer becomes another writer's story.

Don't get the idea that Tom's workshop was always bliss. Certain students wanted overnight success and attacked him when that didn't happen. In recent years a female student accused Tom of favoring his male students, and she campaigned for all of his female students to abandon the workshop.

More recently it came to light that someone at my agent's office—the same agency that represented Tom—had been embezzling for years. Tom's money, Edward Gorey's money, Mario Puzo's money, my money, millions of dollars. So much for my lax checkbook balancing!

The agency folded. The thief went to prison, and the courts could find no money to recover.

This isn't a happy ending, not exactly. But there's always an ending after the ending. That one, I said.

If you were my student I'd ask you to consider just one more possibility.

What if all of our anger and fear is unwarranted? What if world events are unfolding in perfect order to deliver us to a distant joy we can't conceive of at this time?

Please consider that the next ending will be the happy one.

About the Author

Chuck Palahniuk has been a nationally bestselling author since his first novel, 1996's *Fight Club*, was made into the acclaimed David Fincher film of the same name. Palahniuk's work has sold millions of copies worldwide. He lives outside Portland, Oregon.